EASTERN WISDOM
HELPS ENTERPRISE

EASTERN WISDOM HELPS ENTERPRISE

✦

The True Story of a Successful Entrepreneur

John S. Song

iUniverse, Inc.
New York Lincoln Shanghai

EASTERN WISDOM HELPS ENTERPRISE
The True Story of a Successful Entrepreneur

iUniverse, Inc.

For information address:
iUniverse, Inc.
2021 Pine Lake Road, Suite 100
Lincoln, NE 68512
www.iuniverse.com

ISBN: 0-595-30593-8 (pbk)
ISBN: 0-595-76144-5 (cloth)

Printed in the United States of America

Jory, I dedicate this book to you in the hope it will serve as an inspiration throughout your life. I love you forever.

Dad, 2002

Acknowledgments

My wife, Helen, helped me by typing my manuscripts. My son, Jordan, did all the miracle works on the computer. My labor attorney, Carol, checked my manuscript in reference to labor laws. She read the whole book and loved it. Sadly, she has passed away. My financial advisor, Bernie, made sure I did not say anything against the law. My editor, Laurie, made the book possible.

I wish them all healthy, happy, and long lives.

John, 2002

Contents

(1) Chinese proverb: "Failure is the mother of success."

(2) Chinese proverb: "Man without will is like a boat without a rudder."

(3) Confucius said: "Worry about the way, don't worry about being poor."

(4) Confucius said: "When the boss practices benevolence, his people will be happy."

(5) Chinese proverb: "Persistent efforts will yield results."

(6) Confucius said; "When the superior shows sympathy, no subordinate will dare to be disrespectful."

(7) Confucius said: "Zican was generous in caring for his people, and just in employing their services."

(8) Chinese proverb: "Sick people take all chances on doctors."

(9) Confucius said for greatest health and happiness, people should behave in harmony with nature.

(10) Chinese proverb: "Rather make a gentleman an enemy; never make an evil man an enemy."

(1) Chinese proverb: "Accumulate small amounts to amass a large sum."

(2) Confucius said: "Don't worry about not being recognized by others; seek what to do to earn your own recognition."

(3) Chinese proverb: "Action is more powerful than talk."

(4) Confucius said: "Being not able to endure petty unfairness will ruin the major plan."

(5) Confucius said: "If you manage with an upright heart, who dares not to be upright?"

(1) Chinese proverb: "Rivers and mountains can evolve, but human character is difficult to change."

(2) Chinese proverb: "Even the Emperor's officials do not beat a man who is offering a present."

(3) Confucius said: "Every conduct should be in moderation, not to extremes."

(4) Confucius said: "Being generous you will be able to use people effectively."

(5) Confucius said: "The Book of Odes has three hundred poems which can be summed up in one sentence: 'Think no evil.'"

(6) Chinese proverb: "You can cover up the fire, but cannot hide the smoke."

(7) Confucius said: "Looking for petty gains, your important tasks will not be successful."

(8) Chinese proverb: "Petty gains are never worth the effort."

(9) Chinese proverb: "Ten years you lived at the east side of the river, next ten years you lived on the west side of the river." (Ten years, everything might be changed.)

(10) Confucius said: "Bo Yi did not nurse old grudges, so others didn't have ill feeling toward him."

(1) Sunzi wrote in his Art of War: "Knowing your opponent and knowing yourself, you can go into a hundred battles and never be defeated."

(2) Sunzi wrote in Art of War: "In war, we value victory, not long campaign."

(3) Chinese proverb: "True character is revealed in moments of extreme anger."

(4) Confucius said: "If you are tolerant, you will win over many."

(1) Chinese proverb: "Treat people with honesty; gain others' heart with your own heart."

(2) Confucius said: "If on showing someone one corner, he does not come back with the other three, I will not repeat the lesson."

(3) Mencius said: "People should use loyalty as the foundation for doing things."

(4) Chinese proverb: "Well starts and well ends."

(5) Confucius said: "Promote the good and the talented."

(1) Chinese proverb: "One who has will, will succeed."

(2) Chinese proverb: "An able man doesn't make a fixed-amount income."

(3) Confucius said: "Gentleman does not seek petty gains."

(4) Chinese proverb: "Hearing about hundred times is not as good as seeing once."

(5) Mencius said: "To convince people by virtue, people, delighted in their heart, will be sincerely persuaded."

(6) Chinese proverb: "Missing by a hair, result will differ by thousand miles."

(7) Chinese proverb: "Experiencing one event, gains one notch of wisdom."

(8) Chinese proverb: "One inch of time is worth one inch of gold. One inch of gold cannot buy one inch of time."

Introduction

In 1997, I traveled back to China, where I was born and educated. I had not been back, except for a brief visit in 1979, for over forty years, since I moved to the United States to earn a master's degree in engineering. Due to political changes in China at the time, I was unable to launch a business in my homeland, as I had planned. I had the good fortune, however, to spend my lifetime as a successful entrepreneur in the United States.

After an instructive youthful business failure, I started the business from scratch that by 2002 had grown into a still-growing company with a hundred and fifty employees and an annual gross of twenty million dollars.

During my travels in China, I visited the university where I had studied for my undergraduate degree. The highlight of the tour was the Economics and Management School. The university president's assistant guided me through the corridors, where serious-looking students hurried to their classrooms.

"Over ninety percent of the country's top students attend our university," the assistant explained. "Many study for a Master of Business Administration."

An MBA! Such a program had not even existed in my days as a student. Both the university and I had come a long way in the intervening years. I felt inspired to underwrite a scholarship to encourage good students to study for this advanced degree.

When I told the assistant of my intention, he was surprised and pleased. "Please come back next year," he said, "to celebrate the university's anniversary with us, and then, participate in the formal establishment of the MBA scholarship in your name." I accepted his invitation with alacrity.

When the university awarded the MBA scholarships for the first year, I wrote to the leading student a letter of congratulation, and advised him:

"The basic principle of management is for the top management to establish a culture for the organization that encourages scientific studies, exploring modern technologies, innovation and risk-taking, the basic value of Western culture. In the mean time, promote and adopt Eastern wisdom, to hold the virtues of honesty, loyalty, and trustworthiness, the heart of Eastern philosophies. Hiring intelligent employees who can work and live in such a culture, with every one having the same attitude, you will be a great success in business. Since you conduct yourself honestly and loyally, you do not have a guilty conscience. You are open and clean in front of anybody, thus you are happy, and adding exercise, you will also be healthy. At such time, you will be a complete successful man."

"The school teaches Western modern management techniques, such as systems, rules, finance, marketing, training, and so on. These are tangible, quantitative subjects and we will not discuss them in this book. The heart of management is culture which is intangible, and this is what we are focusing on."

"The following four sayings will show you a valuable culture can be created with Eastern wisdom to guide everyone's behavior:

"Confucius said: 'Without trustworthiness, one cannot establish one's self.'—How true!"

"Mencius said: 'Respect the good, use the able.'"

"Sunzi wrote in his *Art of War*: 'The king should not start a war because of anger.' "He implied that we should not take action when we are mad.—How wise!"

"Chinese proverb: 'Spiders busily weave their cobwebs, flying insects will come.' Prepare yourself, your opportunity will come—How useful!"

In this book the writings of problems and solutions are based on actual happenings, and written in story telling narrative for a relaxed and enjoyable reading, with Eastern wisdom sayings to conclude the stories to show the philosophical principles. The happenings have their own particular characters and can be used as management discussing subjects. As the happenings were recorded following the order of their occurrence, the book looks like the autobiography of the author, but actually, they were written only for the purpose of case studies.

For entrepreneurs, a good culture should be established as soon as possible, so that the endeavor can be progressed in the right direction from the very beginning.

By my experience, a successful entrepreneur is driven by a powerful underlying energy, the burning desire to build a business. However, to ensure of having a long range success in business and in life, the essential elements besides hard working are honesty and loyalty, the essence of Eastern philosophy.

Similarly, the success or failure of a company depends basically on the culture of the company. Does the management truly practice honesty, loyalty, and fairness? Does everyone in the organization have a forward-looking attitude, drive aggressively for new things, and work together as one family and comfortably under the company culture. Management must set a positive example, thereby leading others to build a successful establishment.

Perhaps Western readers will be surprised to learn that ancient Eastern wisdom resides comfortably in the modern business environment, and indeed, enhances Western practicality and profit-making potential. The following chapters will demonstrate how this balanced system has worked for me, and can work for you.

1

Growing Water Chestnuts

"Failure is the mother of success."

—Chinese proverb

While China was busy fighting the Japanese invasion in the 1940s, the government continued to allow students to travel abroad for advanced studies at their own expense. I was lucky to be able to come to the United States with a group of about twenty students. At that time the Chinese government allowed us to travel abroad to be educated, as long as we were financially self-sufficient. Their hope was that we would return with our newfound skills and apply them to rebuild our country after the war with Japan.

I enrolled at Cornell University, working for a master of science degree in Industrial Engineering. I planned to go back to China to enterprise after school. I knew that when the war was over, just about every industry would be needed. Which ones, I wondered, would be most suitable for me? What niche could I choose? Certainly the government would run the heavy industries. Most light industries such as textiles, chemicals, paper, and the like were already thriving enterprises my predecessors had built financial empires around.

Finally, I came up with the idea that Chinese foods were always important, and that canning would be a good start. First we would have to have cans, so as soon as I finished school, I applied for a job with a tin-can manufacturing company. I intended to form my own company in China with investments from friends by buying obsolete can manufacturing equipment from the United States or Europe. Once established, we could install modern facilities and add a canning business.

To my amazement, the management of the can company picked up my idea and decided to manufacture cans in China themselves. They approached a successful Chinese businessman in New York City to be a partner in the venture.

1

This man also saw the opportunity as perfect for himself. In a very short time, they signed an agreement to start the China Can Company as soon as the situation there permitted. Naturally, they would consider me as a working member of the new company.

But this was not what I wanted. I had intended to be an entrepreneur. If I wanted to stick to my original plan, I had to think of something other than the can business. This worked in my favor in the long run, because by 1949, the Chinese central government lost the civil war to the communist party, and the China Can Company project was dropped.

In the meantime, however, at loose ends, I took the opportunity to enroll as a graduate student in Business Administration at Columbia University in New York City. By the time I finished my school year at Columbia, my money was practically gone. With a student visa, I was not permitted to take a money-earning job except with a foreign firm, so, ironically, I took a job in the export department of the company owned by the Chinese businessman who wanted to start the China Can Company.

Chinese proverb: "A man without will is like a boat without a rudder."

Time flew. I felt I had to begin building the foundation for my own career. The turmoil in China was preventing the Chinese in America from obtaining many foods normally imported from the Far East. Among these difficult-to-get foods were water chestnuts. The Chinese restaurants paid an extraordinary price for them, particularly for fresh ones, which tasted much better than canned.

On researching the subject, I came up with three leads. I learned that the U.S. Agricultural Department Experimental Station in Savannah, Georgia, had been experimenting for several years with growing water chestnuts in small plots. A Chinese restaurant owner in Savannah grew a little for his own use, and an American farmer in South Carolina was considering cultivating them on his farm. Based on this limited information, I went to Savannah to investigate.

First, I visited the Agricultural Department Experimental Station. The man in charge of the station, Joseph Biset, was an elderly gentleman, plain and sincere. He shared the department's experience with water chestnuts: the climate in Savannah was right for growing them; land and labor were cheap. According to his estimates, one acre could produce nearly twenty thousand pounds per year. The only problem was the composition of Georgia's soil, which had a high percentage of clay. I did not think this would be a problem, because water chestnuts grow in water, and soil with clay retains water.

Next, I visited the small Chinese restaurant in Savannah. The owner, an easygoing man, had grown water chestnuts with the help of a Japanese farmer. They produced only a few bushels a year in a small area for his own use.

My last contact, the farmer in South Carolina owned a small, old-fashioned plantation and turned out to be reluctant to try a new endeavor like growing water chestnuts.

By the time I returned to New York, I had created a success picture in my mind. Farm acreage and labor near Savannah were very cheap compared with other areas, even in the south. If we could produce twenty thousand pounds of water chestnuts per acre, and sell them at the high prices Chinese restaurants were willing to pay, five acres would generate a lot of revenue.

Confucius said: "Worry about the way; don't worry about being poor."

I was desperately looking for a way, and easily justified to myself that water chestnut farming was it. Although I didn't know how to grow water chestnuts, I considered myself a fast learner and a hard worker. With Mr. Biset's help, surely I should be able to do it!

A longtime friend of mine, Mr. S. H. Fu, had become rich from his humble beginning by investing in growth stocks. I proposed my idea to him, and he was impressed with its prospects. He agreed to venture ten thousand dollars, and I would supply the labor. We would share our profit, if and when we had any.

Immediately, I informed Mr. Biset of our decision, and in the late winter of 1950, I drove to Savannah with my personal belongings.

Mr. Biset proved truly helpful, and I trusted his honesty without reservation. He drove me around looking for land, and in a few days, we found a twenty-nine-acre parcel located twelve miles west of Savannah on Highway 80. With more than one thousand feet of frontage, the location was favorable for doing business. The price was considered very low, even in the Savannah area.

Tall weeds and sickly-looking southern pines dotted the land. The western section was somewhat lower than the rest, and muddy even in the dry season of winter. Because of poor drainage, the land probably could not be worked on during the spring rainy period.

The station tested the soil and found it to be acidic. We could apply lime to neutralize it if we started farming in a relatively small area. Presuming we could do something to improve the drainage, I bought the land.

I visited the neighbors. A gentleman who worked in the city lived to the east side, on a small farm separated from ours by a beat-up wooden fence patrolled by an indifferent bull. A cattle farmer and his daughter, a flight attendant, lived to the south. Both households proved genial and supportive. I never met the folks to the west; that border was too swampy to cross. Another wooden fence ran along the highway. I fixed the creaky gate at the entrance.

A well digger recommended by Mr. Biset came to see me at my rented garage apartment in Bloomingdale, a village only a couple of miles from the farm. The minute I saw him, I got the impression he was a strong, down-to-earth, honest man. We shook hands on a deal: for three hundred dollars he would dig a four-hundred-foot well with four-inch pipe. I immediately called a reliable friend in New York to buy a used water pump for me.

Next, I bought a tractor from one of Mr. Biset's friends. This transaction created a little unpleasantness. A man in Bloomingdale sold tractors, and the neighbors criticized me for being dominated by Mr. Biset, who they saw as "the government man at the agricultural station". They thought I should have bought the tractor from the dealer in our own village. Well, what could I say? Such grumbles would pass away in time.

A friendly carpenter, recommended by a fellow from the church, came with his ten-year-old son to build a shed to house the well, pump, and tractor. The shed was located about fifty feet from the main road which was on the higher ground along the east border, midway between the entrance to the north and the south border.

I began the work of clearing land south of the shed for planting, but the tractor often bogged down when it hit a wet spot. A couple of times when I got stuck, the south-side neighbor came out to help. Clearly the land was too swampy to farm and had to be drained, soon.

Mr. Biset introduced me to the county engineer, Mr. Norman Glenn, and asked for his help with drainage. We thought the city might be willing to help, because my success at water chestnut farming would be good for Savannah. The city had little industry, and therefore the economy had not moved forward like other southern cities. Our business, though small, could attract other northern capital investments in the region.

The engineer was a man of few words, and I could not figure him out. But he said he would see what he could do, so I remained hopeful.

About two weeks later, I arrived at the farm at sunup. At the entrance, I saw two human silhouettes standing by the shed, each holding a long stick. As I drew closer, I realized they were prison guards with shotguns watching a chain gang of some twenty African-American convicts digging a ditch. The prisoners were chained together at their ankles so each individual could only move around enough to dig with his shovel. I had seen such things in movies, but never thought they could happen here, with me in the scene.

I greeted the guards, who nodded politely, then turned around and stood at attention like two statues. Mr. Glenn was standing by the road a few yards away. He had already laid out the ditch.

"Good morning!" I said heartily.

"Good morning," he replied, then introduced me to the guards.

The convicts never lifted their heads. For a moment, everyone stood still. Nobody spoke. Occasionally, I heard the clinking sound of the steel chains, when a prisoner moved his feet. Then, the county engineer walked toward his car. I thanked him, and he left.

In a few days, the crew had dug a drainage ditch four feet wide, three feet deep, and over one thousand feet long. It would have cost plenty, if I had done it on my own. The land soon became much improved.

At the time, all farm workers in the area were African-Americans. They worked from sunup to sundown, as long as the light held, and nobody knew or cared about the hour of the day. I hired a young man named Lamar, who was stocky, strong, and short, to help me on the farm. We laid out five acres on the south side of the ditch.

Lamar cut the roots around the scattered trees with an ax, and I drove the tractor to pull them down. In a couple of weeks, we had pulled over twenty small pine trees.

Then I hired Reggie, a big man, to plow the five acres with the tractor. Lamar and I followed the tractor in the burning spring sun, picking up piles and piles of roots and broken stumps.

At sundown they went home, and I headed for the general store to have my regular supper: two thick hamburgers with grilled onion, topped off with a pint of strawberry ice cream, with several cups of tea as chaser. I felt happy with my decisions. I never thought I could have been a professor with a Ph.D., eating delicious Chinese food in comfort. In truth, I was much better off than Lamar, who earned two dollars a day that I was happy to pay him.

Confucius said: "When the boss practices benevolence, his people will be happy."

I wished to follow the teachings of Confucius, and Mr. Biset told me that I was paying the field hands much higher wages than the other local farmers. Still,

Lamar could not afford to buy meat, so he bought bones with some threads of meat left after the meat had been trimmed off. Every day for lunch, he sucked on a boiled bone with a whole loaf of bread and a pint of milk. Reggie did not eat lunch. He drank well water, but I never saw him sweat under the scorching sun.

We cleared five acres, built banks around the outer edges to hold water, and divided the land into one-acre patches with banks in between. The pump hummed, and the water flowed cheerfully into the central trough, which could be swung around to irrigate all the patches. The farm suddenly became full of life, and everything seemed beautiful. A warm feeling filled my body.

Chinese proverb: "Persistent efforts will yield results."

When we were ready to plant the water chestnuts, I hired five women from five neighboring farms. I had to drive twelve miles on country roads before dawn to pick them up. When we arrived at the farm at sunup, everybody started to work without conversation. The women took one break for lunch. When the sun hung low in the west, I drove them home.

One day, one of the women was continuously talking, while the others silently planted the water chestnuts. Somebody told me she was drunk. I hadn't noticed her being drunk that morning, when I picked her up. Nevertheless, I had to take her home before lunch. I felt sorry for her and paid her a full day's wage. Her pay was pitifully low, but again high by local standards.

Confucius said: "When the superior shows sympathy, no subordinate will dare to be disrespectful."

I had been eating at the general store for months and was tired of the owner's hamburgers and ice cream, so I boarded with an old couple who owned a farm and a gas station. The woman often cooked meat with black beans and grits, quite a change for me.

One evening, the old man said, "My boy, I have heard you are overpaying the niggers. That upsets the farm folks here."

I didn't argue with him, but quit boarding with them the next day. How could the workers live on what those farmers paid them? I believed such injustice would be corrected in time, and that the farmers would, somehow, sometime, pay for their greed and prejudice. In the meantime, people were happy to work for me.

Confucius said: "Zican was generous in caring for his people and just in employing their services."

Surprisingly, people in the Old South treated Chinese almost like one of them. If they held a prejudice against someone, they would usually just ignore the person. If they noticed a difference from them, they would pay extraordinary attention to the stranger, being more than usual polite and attentive. On Sundays, when nobody was supposed to work, I went to church with the village folks. People didn't ignore me or pay special attention to me. This made me feel quite at home.

To show my appreciation to Mr. Glenn for having had my ditch dug, I invited him and his wife to a Chinese dinner. They reciprocated by inviting me to their home many times, often for dinner. Mrs. Glenn was a schoolteacher, as nice as a person could be.

I met their two college-age sons. One Saturday evening, I went to their home for dinner and was introduced to a young American lady who had just finished college. I found her to be very attractive, but I felt I was not in a position to think about a girlfriend. I decided that, after a couple of years, if my farm was successful, I would ask Mrs. Glenn to introduce me to her again.

One Sunday after church, I drove to the farm just to look around. Oh, what a beautiful sight it was! Before me lay a blanket of tender green foliage, young, healthy, and thick. Beyond the plants, the open field was dotted with pine trees. The ditch, full of clear water, stretched to the far end of the land.

On a tall tree, far to the west, a great egret perched, whiter than white, looking at me peacefully. Whence had she come? Why to my farm? Although the ditch and the patches were full of water, how could any fish grow there? Somehow, the egret must have found food on the farm, or she wouldn't be there. She surely made the farm livelier and more enchanting. I wished some of my friends could be there to enjoy that serene world. I reluctantly headed homeward, leaving the graceful egret to her solitude.

When everything seems tranquil, the unexpected often occurs. For several days, I had noticed the water in the patches had been partially drained during the night. I checked the banks and found some small holes through which water slowly flowed out. Somehow we had to block the leaks.

The county agent from the Agriculture Department, a thin man in his forties named Henry who always wore a straw hat, stopped by to see how things were going. His job was to visit the farmers in his district and offer help if needed. This man was a clever character, skeptical, the "I-didn't-do-it" type. The first time he came, we had just bought the farm. He looked around, then left, having said nothing; but I knew what was in his mind: He thought Mr. Biset had led me to buy a worthless farm on wet clay.

The second time he came, we were cutting down the tall weeds.

"Georgia weeds follow you," he said with a grin, and tilted back his straw hat. "The moment someone cuts them down, they grow right up behind him."

"You are wasting everybody's time, what you have said does not do any good to me or anyone else." I thought to myself,

The third time he arrived was just when I had discovered the water-draining problem.

He studied the holes on the banks and said, "John, these holes are dug by crawfish. They work at night. Not much you can do about it."

"We have to do something," I said.

He gave it some thought. "Catfish love crawfish. If you put some catfish in the water, they might eat the crawfish." Then he shrugged and left.

I didn't think he had noticed the whiter-than-white egret on the tall pine tree. He didn't look skeptical either, though, now that he had seen the water chestnuts growing in the finely defined patches.

I called Mr. Biset for his advice.

"Until we think of some better way to handle the crawfish," Mr. Biset said, "there's no harm in putting some catfish in there." After a moment, he continued, "I know a friend who can get you catfish. I'm sure he won't charge you for that."

Chinese proverb: "Sick people take all chances on doctors."

I was willing to take a chance on a long shot. I went to see Mr. Biset's friend. The man owned a tavern on the shore of a branch of the Savannah River, north of the city. He led me through the back door of his tavern to a small motorboat docked behind the building. To my mystification, he loaded an old crank-handle telephone and two butterfly nets in the boat, but no fishing poles or nets. After we boarded, he started the motor and guided the boat slowly and quietly up the river.

What a deserted river! The still water flowed unnoticeably against us. In about ten minutes, we reached a narrow spot. He turned the boat around and stopped the motor. I heard no birds and saw no insects. The water was colored bronze by the dead leaves and branches beneath the surface, and the thick bushes on both banks sent branches into the water. A dense canopy of trees blocked most of the sunlight. I found it very spooky, and thought the underworld must be like this. I would have been scared, if I'd been there alone.

He dropped the telephone wire into the water. When it reached the bottom, he started to crank the handle of the telephone box, as if we were making an old-fashioned phone call.

"Get a net and get ready to catch fish," he instructed me.

What fish? I wondered. But all of a sudden, flashing silver fins broke the surface, as dozens of fish splashed in circles, shocked and dazed by the electric current he had sent through the water. I scooped up some fish with the net and plunked them into a pail of water he had in the boat. He used another net and caught more fish than I did.

After five minutes, he started his motor again, and we sailed down river with a pail full of catfish. Back at his tavern, he said to me, "You can take the pail." I thanked him and left. Later I learned it was illegal to fish with an electrical apparatus.

I hurried to the farm and slipped the twenty-eight catfish into the water of the patches. They disappeared immediately. The next morning, I drove to the farm and, to my disappointment, the catfish had not eaten the crawfish. The crawfish had dug more holes in the banks.

Nobody ever saw the catfish again, dead or alive. Had the egret eaten them? I wondered. Every morning I would block up the holes in the banks by hand. I never told Henry, the county agent, that I had tried the catfish solution and failed. I hated to give him the satisfaction.

One day, I came to the farm and found my neighbor's bull on my side of the fence, eating weeds. I took a long pole and tried to chase him back. To my surprise, he lowered his head, bent his two front legs, and got ready to charge. I ran toward my neighbor's house and yelled for help. He called his bull back to his side of the fence right away.

Another day, while digging a stump, I stepped on an ants' nest. The ants scurried up my legs inside my trousers.

"Ants in my pants!" I cried out.

Lamar yelled back, "Jump in the ditch!"

I immediately immersed my lower body in the water of the ditch, stripped off my pants, and saved my legs. How could I have made it known to the ants that I didn't intentionally destroy their home? I apologized to them inwardly as I soaked.

Confucius said for greatest health and happiness, people should behave in harmony with nature.

These incidents taught me a lesson: Never tangle with anyone who cannot control himself, even if you are right. If a man is mentally off, don't argue with him. If a man is drunk, don't try to reason with him. If a man is thick, why debate with him? Some people turn into monsters as soon as they get behind a steering wheel. Avoid arguing with them, even if they are violating the traffic law.

Chinese proverb: "Rather make a gentleman an enemy; never make an evil man an enemy."

The crop had fully grown. I invited Mr. Fu, my investor friend from New York, to come down and see what had been accomplished. Of course, he could never imagine how much labor and thought had been put into the farm. Apparently satisfied to see the green field, he returned to New York with two southern baked apple pies.

A couple weeks after Mr. Fu left, we found some brownish spots in the foliage. Mr. Biset suggested we apply lime to the soil to neutralize the acidity. I hired a large platform truck and hauled a full truckload of lime from South Carolina. We spread the lime powder shovel by shovel into the patches. The wind blew the white powder all over the field.

At the most awkward moment, Henry stopped by to say hello again. He surveyed the whole situation, pushed back his straw hat, and said, "This is just a drop in the bucket."

He actually was right, but his remark infuriated me. Why offer negativity instead of some tangible assistance? Perhaps Henry was resentful of Mr. Biset's influence over me, but Biset was wholeheartedly behind me, right or wrong. What had Henry, as county agent, ever done on my behalf?

A few weeks later, the crop seemed to be fairly healthy after all. The plants, over three feet tall, were green and thick, covering the five patches like carpets. Water chestnuts were solidly packed in the soil underneath the green foliage. We partially drained the water and left the nuts in the mud.

When harvest time came, we tried to dig the nuts out with shovels. They were trapped in the clayish soil so tight, the mud would not crack open. When we slammed a shovel into the ground, the blade cut many nuts; yet we could not even pry the half-cut nuts from the mud. Even if we'd had a water buffalo to pull a hoe, the soil could not be broken up.

The tractor could not work in the mud, so we drained the patches completely and let the soil partially dry. Then we tried to plow the soil with the tractor, but the result was about the same as using the shovel. We had underestimated the gluing power of Georgia dirt!

Failure and frustration overwhelmed me. "How" I asked myself, "how can we get them out?"

Mr. Biset was depressed over our inability to harvest the crop.

I urged myself on. "We should not give up so easily," I told myself. "We must try to think of some other options." But what options did we have? Business is like a chain; every link must be strong. Our weak link was harvesting. I had been so eager to find my way in the beginning, that I had neglected to investigate how to harvest the easily bruised water chestnuts from clayish soil, before I jumped into the adventure.

The experimental station had had only a very small plot, which they had filled with sandy loam. The nuts were easily picked in the dirt. No one at the agricultural station had considered the effect of the clayish soil either.

I didn't worry about the reaction of my loyal Savannah friends, when they learned I was quitting and going home, but I hated to think the good-for-nothing Henry would have the final laugh.

After I had used up Mr. Fu's investment, I had borrowed money from another friend in New York. The sale of the farmland should bring in enough money to pay back the loan, but what would I say to Mr. Fu?

I had to dispose of the tractor. I went to see the tractor dealer, who was very rude when he learned I was leaving, a totally different person from when he sold me the tractor. He told me with a straight face, "I will repossess the tractor if you fail to pay on time."

"I'm not going to let you take advantage of me." I said to myself. I went back to Bloomingdale and gave the tractor to a farmer who agreed to take over the monthly payments. Naturally, he was delighted and thanked me sincerely.

Next, I made arrangements with a couple of realtors to sell the land. I packed the hand tools in my car, drove to the experimental station, and gave them to Mr. Biset. I said goodbye to my friend and his workers at the station.

From there, I drove to the farm for my last look. It was late in the morning. The water chestnuts plants were still healthy and beautiful. The water trough, the ditch, and the egret on the pine tree all stood poised as if nothing had happened. I bid goodbye to them all.

I encountered little traffic on my way back to New York. The sound of the wheels became so monotonous that by afternoon I grew sleepy. I turned into a drive-in movie theater, parked my car behind the big screen, and took a nap. Nobody would ever suspect that somebody was asleep there, I thought. After the nap, I felt a little happier. "Failure is the mother of success," I said to myself. "Next time, I'll examine every link of the business."

I drove past sunset, then, stopped at a rooming house for travelers. After a hearty dinner at a truck stop, I took a walk. To my surprise, I did not feel bad about the misadventure. I had proven to myself that I was able and willing to take on any task. I also had the nerve and energy to deal with whatever happened. Next time, I promised myself, I would be successful.

2

Saving Money

"Accumulate small amounts to amass a large sum."

—Chinese proverb

I returned to New York to deliver the bad news to Mr. Fu. My investor-friend seemed to understand the situation and didn't give any indication of blaming me, but he didn't try to comfort me, either. He still seemed to have no idea how hard I had worked! With little money left, I started to look for a job.

Most Chinese college graduates could not master the English language, and many had not lived in the United States long enough to know the American way of doing business. They often worked for consulting firms with diminished responsibility. I preferred to work for a regular corporation in order to gain practical experience and hope for advancement opportunities. I would have to have a lot of savings before I would be able to start my own business.

I answered an advertisement from a meat packing company looking for an engineer. My appointment for interview was at noon in a Manhattan hotel room. The interviewer introduced himself and offered me a seat. The moment I sat down, the doorbell rang, and a room service waiter came in carrying a tray, which he set on a small table near the bed.

The host sat at the table, opened the white cloth napkin, and spread it over his lap. He took the metal cover off the dinner plate and picked up a knife and a fork. Before he started working on a large sirloin steak, he lifted his head, looked at me, and asked me a couple of questions. But most of the time, he concentrated on the meat. I felt he had no intention of hiring a Chinese immigrant with a master's degree in industrial Engineering.

I applied for another job with a reputable corporation. Before the interview, I had to take an intelligence test. I needed so much time to read the questions that I finished only half the test before my time was up. I didn't even get an interview.

Finally, through an employment agency, I got a job as a product designer working in the New York sales office of a metal fabricating company in Indiana.

A few months later, they transferred me to the Indiana main plant, and this brought me luck. First, I earned my citizenship, having lived in the United States long enough according to the law. Then the realtor sold the farm in Georgia at twice the original price. With that money, I immediately paid off my debt with interest to my friend in New York who had helped me after Mr. Fu's money had been exhausted. I didn't receive enough money to pay back my investor, but if I had, I would have reimbursed him, too, although the original agreement did not call for it.

As soon as I felt settled with a paying job, I began to think about my family. I had lost contact with them, when I got to the United States, and for several years I could not find out what had happened to my parents. After the Japanese surrendered, the civil war had become truly ferocious. Eventually the communists had conquered the whole country, and the central government had retreated to the province of Taiwan.

Finally, through a schoolmate in Hong Kong, I found an old family friend from our hometown, Mr. Zhou, who was in the antiques business in Hong Kong and was, therefore, allowed to travel to Beijing. I immediately sent a small amount of money to Mr. Zhou and asked him to forward it to my father.

A few months later, Mr. Zhou wrote that he had found my parents in Beijing. They had been lucky enough to escape from the local disturbances to the city, but were penniless. He had handed the money to my father in person during a buying trip to Beijing. Mr. Zhou also mentioned that my brother was working for the new local government and was having trouble with his wife. Later, I figured that was why my father never mentioned my brother in his letters and my brother never wrote me either.

When I arrived in Indiana in 1952, I began to make more money, so I sent a larger sum home. I received a letter from my father, forwarded from Hong Kong, saying both he and my mother felt that no matter what happened, they would be all right. He ended the letter by saying, "Taking care of yourself is of utmost importance." He did not mention what had happened during the years past.

Immediately following this letter, I received another, telling me that they had received the money, and it was like sweet rain after a long drought. He said, "We do not need much. Just periodically send some, and that will be enough for us to survive and we will have no more suffering."

In 1955, I received the sad news from our friend Mr. Zhou that my father had passed away. A couple of years later, my mother left the world. Just at the time when I was making enough money to offer them a better living, they left me! This has hurt me deeply throughout my life.

The metal-fabricating company assigned me to the engineering department as one of six product designers under the direction of a chief engineer.

My coworkers were young fellows, except for one old hand who acted like a group leader. During breaks, everybody gathered around his desk with a cup of coffee and carried on a seemingly exciting conversation.

I thought I should be sociable and join the crowd. I walked to the gathering empty-handed, as there was no tea, and I didn't drink coffee. They were discussing basketball games and players, which I knew nothing about. I listened politely until the break was over, but I felt quite out of place.

A few days later, I tried to join them again. They were talking about cars. I had never paid much attention to cars. I thought a car was for transportation, so I'd learned little about the different models and features. What could I say? I stood there like a dummy. After that, I decided just to stay in my chair during coffee time.

Confucius said: "Don't worry about not being recognized by others; seek what to do to earn your own recognition."

At my drafting board, I could not help but pick up the pencil and fiddle with minor changes. I certainly did not intend to impress anyone. A senior engineer, always well dressed with his hair combed high in the front, did not share my opinion. Early one day, I had just set up my desk and board, when he walked into the office. He and I were alone.

He strode to my desk and, in a low voice, said, "John, I notice you work all the time. You know you don't have to work that hard. Are you trying to make all of us look bad, or are you working for a promotion?"

I looked him straight in the eye and said firmly, "I work because I feel like working. That certainly is none of your business. I don't give a damn what you do."

Other people had begun to come in. My answer did not seem to surprise or anger him. He had probably expected that kind of rebuke. After that, I acted as if nothing had ever happened, and never mentioned the incident to anyone; and, likewise, he talked to me as usual.

Possibly my hard working had made an impression, though, for when the company started an Impact Extrusion Department, which worked on extruding aluminum containers by impact, the management assigned me to it.

Chinese proverb: "Action is more powerful than talk."

Several months passed, and the new department had not done well. One time, we had a technical problem no one could solve, including the man in charge, the young engineer, and the pressman. Although I had no previous experience in impact extrusion, I believed technical theories should apply and came up with an idea worth considering. I offered the suggestion to Jerry Stewart, the department head.

He looked at me for several moments, then said jokingly, "If you are so smart, why aren't you a millionaire?"

Astonished, I smiled and walked out of his office. He must have thought my idea ridiculous. Perhaps his remark was one of his standard phrases. Nevertheless, he should have offered some responsible answer. Later, I learned that his department had failed and was closed.

This company was not large. The president was a friendly man who talked and joked with all the employees. Everyone thought he was particularly nice and taking good care of me, except me. He paid me as little as he could get away with, and I never wanted to ask for a raise.

I felt management should pay what an employee is worth, without being asked. If they don't, the employee will leave. Because I believed the company wasn't paying me appropriately, I went to Chicago and found a much better job as a blank development department head with a small company making aircraft aluminum forgings. My job was to design and make the aluminum blank plate to be forged into the wanted part.

I gave two weeks' notice to the president, who responded, "We were just discussing your salary and planning to give you a hundred-dollar raise."

"Thanks," I replied, "but I have already given my word."

I may be giving the impression that I devoted my life entirely to work, but that was not the case. When I stayed at International House, in uptown Manhattan, a friend had introduced me to European folk dance. Soon folk dancing became a favorite way for me to relax. When I moved to the Midwest, I could not find a convenient folk dancing group, so I joined a square-dance group. At one dance, I met a beautiful girl named June, and we started going bicycling and canoeing.

Before we knew it, my square-dance partner and I were getting married in a beautiful old church, near where June used to work. We held the reception in a nearby restaurant. Everything about the ceremony was American. I even fed a piece of wedding cake to my bride, and she did likewise for me.

I had known a few Chinese students who had married American girls, and as far as I could see, their marriages were successful. As for me, I found it necessary to make a lot of adjustments to the role of an American husband.

For instance, one evening my wife and I had dinner with two American couples from June's art group. After the dinner, I offered to pay the bill, but they insisted upon sharing the expense.

On our way home after the dinner, June asked, "Why did you offer to pay for everybody's dinner?"

"I felt odd that everyone paid for their own food," I replied.

"That's Chinese custom. Americans don't do that unless we invite them to dinner as our guests," June explained.

When we first got married, my in-laws invited us to their house for dinner the following Sunday. Their home was not large, but they had a beautiful dining table and used a full set of porcelain with pink flowers. June helped her mother serve fried chicken with mashed potatoes and gravy, green beans, and rhubarb pie, which was June's favorite dessert. Nearly every Sunday we were invited back for the same dinner.

After we bought our house in the western suburbs, June asked her parents to come every Sunday for country-fried chicken with her famous mashed potatoes. Finally, I suggested, "Next Sunday, can we invite your parents to dinner in Chinatown? Afterwards, we can go to Brookfield Zoo to walk around a little." As it turned out, they really enjoyed that day.

In China, the husband determines the social activities, but in America, the wife usually makes the social arrangements, so our activities were usually with June's American friends. Before long the only Chinese friends we saw were two close friends of mine, and my niece's family. Later, when we had our own business, we added many business friends, who were all Americans. Consequently, I became a fully Americanized man.

My next boss was a hardworking entrepreneur. Art Kohl owned a successful die shop and had seen an opportunity in forging aircraft components. He started a forging company as a new venture, but at that point in his life, he did not wish to work hard anymore. Instead, he relied on two associates, Don and David Peterson.

Don had been the foreman at Mr. Kohl's die shop, but he knew nothing about forging and did not intend to learn. He did not understand management, either, although he had the title of vice president. He just walked around and did practically nothing.

David, a newly hired general manager, a sensible and able man, ran the whole operation. Forging blank development was for most part a trial-and-error process. I enjoyed the work, mainly because I had the responsibility of producing the right blanks.

Our working hours were from eight o'clock to five, with one hour for lunch. I usually came in a little earlier, and always worked hard.

Mr. Kohl usually left home at noon, went to the same restaurant every day for brunch, washed down his steak with some hard liquor, and arrived at his office by about three o'clock, when he would immediately ask to try the newly developed forging blanks. Since we knew his schedule, we usually had the blanks ready for him. We would finish the trial by five o'clock, and make any needed changes in the blank design the next day.

One time, after an initial trial, he wanted to make modifications to the blanks and try them again before going home. That would take several more hours. I told him I had come in before eight o'clock, worked hard all day, was tired, and planned to go home at five. Either he ignored me or didn't hear me.

The next day, the press operator told me the boss had looked for me the evening before and had become very angry, when he found out I had left. I knew he must be furious, but would get over it quickly. He knew he wasn't fair to his employees, but he would cover it up with his charming smile, when he wanted to use it. I called that dishonesty.

Equally revolting was his close associate, Don, who, during a staff meeting, levered his right leg onto the armrest of his high-back vinyl executive chair and cut his nails. What an ugly sight! He let the nail cuttings fly all over his desk, clothes, and floor. How long could any company survive with a drunken president and a crude vice-president?

The aluminum aircraft forging business must have filled a valuable niche at that time, as a large eastern company bought Mr. Kohl out and built a new plant in a western suburb, retaining his staff to run the enlarged company.

Everything had just gotten started after the move, when David Peterson quit. I took one look at the replacement and knew he was rotten from the inside out. Small with an insincere smile, he appeared to be an uneducated low-down character. His conversations always wound up with crass stories about girls. I thought he must be a sex maniac or mentally sick.

One day, the president called me to his office and questioned me about a project on a large piece of forging. I explained it would not be possible to produce such a large and complicated part in one operation. He did not like my answer and told me to try harder.

I didn't appreciate that remark; I always worked hard. I became angry and lost my head. I stormed out of his office, stomped down the steps to the factory cement floor, and threw the forging on the floor like a bowling ball. It slid all the way to the other end of the building. I walked slowly toward the forging, but was stopped by the white-haired plant guard.

"John, take it easy. Slow down," he counseled. "If you are not here, everything will go on just as it is."

I took a deep breath and thanked him. After a few more steps, I cooled down. I knew I shouldn't let myself get so mad or throw things around. I also knew I was overtired and irritable, but even so, taking it easy and slowing down did not seem to be part of my nature. I thought the plant guard must have been taking it easy and slowing down all his life. That was why, at his old age, he still had to take on a simple job as a plant guard. Nevertheless, he made me begin to wonder what I should do next.

I began looking for a new job. This time, I found work easily as a research engineer at the research and development group of the can company that had given me a one-year training program at its production plants a few years before. Because our relationship had not been very good, and because I had not learned much about can manufacturing in their so-called training program, I didn't mention my previous employment with them. No matter, at such a large company, the left hand does not know what the right hand has done.

My new environment could not have been more different from the rough and tough forging outfit. The manager placed me with two other men in one office. One had a Ph.D. in food technology, and the other was an older and much experienced chemical scientist. Both men were kind, sincere, and helpful, and they taught me a lot about packaging development. I truly respected them and treated them like my own older brothers.

To start me off, they assigned me to work for a director in charge of tin can testing. I came to realize that tin can manufacturing involved a great deal of technology. After a couple of years, I was transferred to general packaging, then settled down at the plastic-fitting group. At that time, in the mid-1950s, plastics were new to most people, even at the research and development group.

The various departments of this research and development group won, on average, more than one hundred patents a year, and during the next two years I came up with a few patents, most of which were neither practical nor useful. Usually none of them reached the development stage. Rarely did people expend effort on others' patents, and seemingly nobody really cared.

Once, I got a packaging idea I thought could be useful. I made a sketch and showed it to my boss, the director of the section. He looked at it carefully and said, "It will never work. Leave it here, and let me think more about it." He put my sketch in his file drawer. A year later, he obtained a patent based on my sketch. I just laughed inside and told no one.

Confucius said: "Being not able to endure petty unfairness will ruin the major plan."

When I became supervisor of product design in plastic fittings and packaging, we had several engineers working exclusively on new plastic closures and spouts for tin cans. We searched domestic and foreign patents and tried to develop ideas ourselves.

One man, a Mr. Malnati, called on me for plastic product work. He came from a small plastic molding shop and had contacts within the research and development group. People called him "The Talker" for obvious reasons. Whenever he had lunch with us in the cafeteria, people would turn around and stare, because his voice was so high and loud.

Mr. Malnati had been impressed by my work, and he proposed that I went to work for his company to develop new products. He offered me a two percent royalty for my inventions. As he was the vice president of this molding company and the company was small and simple, I thought we might be able to accomplish something together. I accepted his offer and notified my boss. The group gave me a farewell party on a Friday evening, and I reported to work at the molding company the following Monday.

The Talker introduced me to the owner, who told me that his company could not give me royalties for my inventions. I asked The Talker blankly, "Why didn't you tell me this last week, so I didn't quit my job?"

He lowered his eyes, and offered no answer.

I would have liked nothing better than to walk out of his shop, but I could not afford to do that. As I left that conference, I thought the situation has changed, and I have to start preparations for my own business right away.

I didn't tell anyone except June about this betrayal. She guessed the royalty idea had been The Talker's, and the president had overruled him. Of course, I made a mistake by not asking The Talker to put the agreement in writing.

Confucius said: "If you manage with an upright heart, who dares not to be upright?"

The Indiana boss was greedy, the forging company boss was a slave driver, the can company department boss stole my patent, and the molding shop vice president lied about my royalty. I had had enough examples of what kind of boss not to be. These men were not benevolent, and in the end all failed in business, health, and happiness. In the meantime, though, I had to think of my own future.

The Talker added a drafting board in my office, but I only drew whatever he requested; I offered no ideas of my own. After a few months, he reassigned me to the job of quality control and customer service. I checked the quality of complicated molded products and worked with customers on new projects, and whatever problems they had.

The Talker brought me with him on business visits, though I wasn't sure why, since I was never allowed to participate in the discussions. Finally, I realized that he needed someone educated and knowledgeable to prop up his ego. He was quite intelligent, but had an inferiority complex, because he had never finished high school.

After about two years, he found a new companion, an old buddy of his, whom he hired as a consultant. Now he did not need me anymore. I knew I had to accelerate the preparations to start a business of my own.

3

Getting Money

"Without trustworthiness a man cannot establish himself."

—Confucius

Since the failure of the water chestnut venture, I had been seriously saving money, and after my marriage, June and I worked together to accumulate startup capital for a business of our own. We went out for dinner only once a week, on Saturday evenings, at a nearby family-style restaurant. They served meat loaf, pot roast, fried chicken, and sometimes beef stew. I felt sorry we couldn't go to fashionable restaurants once in a while, but June said she liked casual meals. I had faith in my future, and June had faith in me.

I had to decide what business I'd enter. I wanted something with large potential. I didn't want to run a Chinese restaurant, because the success or failure would depend on the talents, loyalty, and health of the chef. Another possibility was to manufacture and market a needed product, but this route would be very difficult for me, as I had very little capital, and venture capitalists would not be interested unless I had a revolutionary idea, which I did not.

Manufacturing a product might not be too difficult, but marketing and selling merchandise could be very risky. If the product was an industrial item, it might be easier to sell to only a few large companies. If it was a consumer item, I would have to advertise and let people know I had the product. Nobody could be sure the public would like it.

Some inventors develop useful consumer products, and let manufacturers produce them, and the retail giants sell them. This is possible only when the merchandise had been patented and protected. I could imagine a new business going broke, if the product was inferior or not needed.

In the end, I felt custom plastic molding would be my best choice. A molding shop is basically a service business, and it's always easier to sell a service than a product. Also, I knew something about the field, having worked on designs of plastic fittings for tin cans for a few years at the research and development group, and experienced the ins and outs at the plastic molding shop for over two years.

One big plus in operating a custom molding service would be continuity. When a company needed a plastic component for its finished product, it would want that part until the design was changed or a new model made.

Custom molding would leave me free to develop new accounts, while the machine made the parts. Getting new jobs, while keeping old ones, would mean growth. Once my business was established, I could take risks to invent and develop new products. If they were not successful, I could adopt a conservative position and wait for opportunities to develop again. Proceeding in such a manner, our future would be unlimited.

At that time, over thirty plastic molding shops operated in and around the Chicago area. Could I do better than the competition and prosper? I didn't want to compete with the low-end molding business; only the biggest companies could make money by cutthroat pricing for low-margin commodity items. If I stayed at the high-end, producing complicated items, I might be able to surpass the competitors, provided I could do the difficult jobs and finance modern equipment. I decided not to pay much attention to competitors. Instead I would concentrate on doing a better job than they did.

After discussing all these possibilities with June, we decided to start our business with custom plastic molding. Since we'd produce plastic parts or components for other companies, we would require molding machines and accessory equipment to do the job. Because we intended to go for the high-end business, our machines and equipment had to be up to date. Thus, even in the beginning, we needed a relatively large amount of capital. I felt confident, and all I had to do was figure out where to get the money.

Just as I was thinking about finding capital for my business, a friend of mine asked me to invest in his company, an indoor-plant fertilizer business in his home, because he needed cash.

"You have an established business and must have a bank and credit," I said to him over lunch. "Why don't you borrow from the bank? That way nobody will share the ownership of your business."

"I can't," he replied. "The bank wants me to mortgage our house, and I swore I would never do that. I want my wife to have a roof over her head, no matter what happens."

"If you are not confident enough about your own business to pledge your house," I told him frankly, "then, who will trust you to give you money?"

He looked surprised.

"You can't ask other people to take a chance on you when you yourself won't risk what you have," I concluded.

Naturally, I did not invest money in his business, as I needed the funds for my own business. He left disappointed.

Confucius said: "A gentleman makes demands on himself; a petty person makes demands on others."

From this experience, I came to believe even more firmly that I had to put up everything I had before I asked anyone else to invest in me. When people put up money for a new venture, they are motivated by their faith in the person who will be running the business, not for the business itself, about which they know nothing.

If I do not demonstrate a total faith in myself, I thought, how can my friends and relatives trust me with their money, no matter how convincing my proposal?

Then as now, for a salaried man to save much money was very difficult, particularly when the salary was not very high. Nevertheless, during the two years at the plastic molding shop, I had managed to add to my savings. The total amount I put up for my venture convinced people that I was serious about going into business for myself.

Of course, I could figure on June's personal savings, some investment by my father-in-law, and some help from my dear friend Joseph Wang, who had been my classmate in college. But that would not be enough.

I was wary of entering into a partnership. I knew three men who had started a plastic molding company in Chicago a few years before I started to plan my venture. When their business had become somewhat established, two partners felt the third one, who did the selling, was not contributing his share of work and did not deserve to share the profits. Within two years, they forced him to relinquish his shares.

A few years later, the company began to make good money, and one partner started to play. First he played tennis and golf, and later, he played girls. The other poor guy had to work frantically to keep the business going. He wanted out, but the playing partner wouldn't buy his shares at a reasonable price and wouldn't sell his, either.

Such situations are common, even in a husband-and-wife business. Everyone has different opinions, habits, and attitudes toward life. Most people struggle hard together in the beginning, but can run into difficulties when prosperity leads to greed.

Chinese proverb: "To share in hardship is easy; to share in prosperity is hard."

In order to prevent possible future problems, I decided not to allow active partners in my company. Two of my engineer friends wanted to invest in the venture, and although I was desperate for funds, I turned them down. They would have expected to play an active role in my enterprise.

All the investors understood and were happy to be stockholders, not active partners. My father-in-law put part of his retirement savings into my business. My classmate, Joe Wang, believed I would succeed, but his investment stemmed from his friendship for me. Wally, the tool room foreman at the plastic molding shop, had been cordial to me, and he also wanted to invest. I accepted, although I knew he had an ulterior motive: He hoped I would be able to hire his son.

One of my former bosses, a solid engineer from Switzerland, was a very straightforward and honest man. He had always liked me, but I was surprised when he invested in my venture.

Confucius said: "By examining oneself, if there is nothing to be ashamed of, why be worried or troubled?"

A clear conscience for me is healthy, and I knew I had behaved honorably with my wealthy friend in New York, Mr. Fu. I hated to ask him to invest in me again after my failed water chestnut venture nearly ten years before, but my personal resources were exhausted, and I still did not have enough capital to start the business.

So, I reluctantly called Mr. Fu. I reminded him that the water chestnut project had proved me able and honest. I had done many extraordinary things to raise a good crop, and I had paid my debt.

He was not impressed. When I asked him for money, he said, "I'll think about it."

I called him twice more and assured him I would get business, even in the beginning, by working on subcontract jobs. I wanted to add, "Remember, I am your friend. We have been friends for over thirty years. Now I need your help." But I didn't, because by this time, I realized he did not know what friendship is.

In New York, for many years, Mr. Fu and I had gone to Chinatown together every Sunday to eat Chinese noodles for lunch. Even for a leisurely lunch, he was always well dressed, well mannered, and polite, but he never spoke about his past, his daily life, or what he had done the day before. He talked about stocks, but never his own investments. He was so secretive that I sometimes wondered if he really considered me a personal friend. I believe he maintained this same distance from everybody.

I telephoned him one last time, and he agreed to invest a fixed moderate amount. I knew the only reason he finally agreed was to stop my persistent telephone call.

Chinese proverb: "If you are not in want, you can be firm."

I was so desperately in want of money, I accepted Mr. Fu's offer. At that moment, I thought, just to make money for him, I must succeed! I took Mr. Fu's money without a feeling of friendship, but in good faith, for I seriously intended to make money for him.

Next, I went to a local bank to inquire about getting a loan. The officer of the Commercial Loan Department, Byron O'Connor, appeared to be sincere, down-to-earth, and helpful. I told him and his boss, the senior vice president, about my background.

"Probably we can work with you to get a loan guaranteed by the government agency for small business," Mr. O'Connor said. "How much do you want to borrow?"

"Thirty thousand," I replied.

"All right," Mr. O'Connor said. "I'll have the agency send us loan applications."

Two weeks later, we received the forms, three legal-sized sheets printed on both sides. I wrote all the answers on separate blank papers, and after corrections, revisions, and spelling checks by June, I printed the answers neatly on the forms. It took me all day Saturday and Sunday.

I brought the finished forms to the bank early the next Monday morning, and Mr. O'Connor sent the papers to the agency right away.

I waited and waited for what seemed to be a very long time. After three weeks, Mr. O'Connor received a phone call from a man at the agency who told him I had filled out the wrong forms and he would send a new set. I spent the next weekend completing the new application.

Another three weeks passed before Mr. O'Connor heard from the man at the agency. They wanted a detailed plan indicating the anticipated sales and profits for the first three years of my business. Mr. O'Connor, the vice-president, and I looked at each other, puzzled. My business was to be only a small service company. It would be impossible to figure out the sales and profits.

"John," Mr. O'Connor finally said quietly, "try to do the best you can."

I said to them flatly, "I will need an accountant to help me make such a plan. Can you recommend one?"

They recommended a young man who had just taken over a small local accounting firm after the death of his boss.

The young accountant and I worked many hours, guessing at what figures would please the man at the agency to make the approval of the loan guarantee easier. Finally we decided to use:

First year-Revenue $200,000; Profit after tax $20,000
Second year-Revenue $300,000; Profit after tax $30,000
Third year-Revenue $450,000; Profit after tax $45,000

We explained in a footnote that the figures were estimates, based on my expectation that I could get jobs from the many packaging managers of the large corporations, I'd met while working with the can company's research and development group.

This time, the man at the agency was very prompt. He called Mr. O'Connor to ask me to secure letters from the potential corporation customers stating they intended to do business with me.

This was a very big order. Was all this really necessary for a small custom molding shop trying to borrow thirty thousand dollars? Certainly no corporation would give me business right away. How could I ask my friends to write such letters? A letter would have to pass through their corporate bureaucratic channels, and most likely their bosses would not approve.

I began to wonder if the man at the agency was following government rules or just inventing more requirements to discourage me. I promised to myself: "You want me to quit? I'll never quit."

I had no choice but to try to get the letters. I could only explain to my packaging friends that the letters were a mere formality for a loan guarantee application for a government agency. No one would pay attention to the letters later on, and the letters would not obligate them to use my service.

One friend, a true gentleman, said, "John, I'll stick my neck out with or without anybody's approval." So he wrote a letter for me.

Another friend from a large corporation did not hold a responsible position, but still wanted to write a letter to help. "I know you will make it; why not go with a winner?" he told me.

A third letter was promised but never delivered. This friend later told me frankly that he really was not in a position to write such a letter. I appreciated his honesty.

Thus I was able to forward two promising letters to the man at the agency. A month later, he sent the complete file to the bank and asked us to make some corrections and changes. The bankers and I thought the loan guarantee was near being approved. I made the changes the man wanted, returned the file to the agency, and waited.

In only two weeks, the man at the agency called and informed the bankers that the loan had actually been approved. The last hurdle was the FBI; the agency had sent my file to the Washington bureau for investigation. It took another two months for the FBI to clear my case.

It had taken us more than six months to borrow thirty thousand dollars. When I finally received the check, I held it in my hand, smiled, and said aloud, "Perseverance, man, perseverance! Never give up. That's what positive mental attitude is all about."

Chinese proverb: "If you have perseverance, everything will work out."

I had collected a total of eighty-three thousand dollars, enough to get our business started.

One evening after supper, I said to June, "We need a name for the company, one that sounds good but means nothing, so I can do any business I wish under that name."

Right away she said, "How about Magenta?"

"What does magenta mean?" I asked.

"It's a color I like," she explained. June loved to paint in oil.

I didn't know the word.

She showed me the color, and I liked it, too. I looked in the dictionary and didn't find any other meaning, except that Magenta was a town in Italy. We thought it unlikely that such a rare word would have been used already by another company. So without further review, we chose Magenta as our company name and magenta as our company color.

4

Starting My Own Business

Those who take risks are stuffed; those who are afraid are starved."

—Chinese proverb

June and I headed into the winter of 1968 on a hopeful note. We had amassed enough capital to start Magenta, designed our logo and letterhead, and felt very positive about how everything had fallen in place for us. Now Magenta needed a home.

In the late 1960s, most manufacturing businesses were moving from Chicago to the northwest suburbs. The property tax in Chicago was higher than in the suburbs, and most industrial buildings in Chicago had become old. Companies had difficulty finding large plants in the city, while in the suburbs modern industrial parks were being developed, and owners could choose the location and size of their building.

Most important, the price of real estate in the suburbs was lower than in the city, and the land would ultimately be a good investment. The growth in the suburbs had begun, so the property value would surely increase.

I, however, saw many disadvantages for small companies in the suburbs at that time. Suburbanites were mostly middle class, because low-income people could not afford to relocate from Chicago. The suburban houses and apartments were in demand, mostly new, and expensive. Not many people would work at low-paying unskilled jobs, like those I would have to offer in a plastic molding shop. Some housewives looked for work, but they didn't like to take on night-shift hours, between midnight and eight o'clock. A friend of mine who had his molding plant in a western suburb could not hire enough third-shift workers to run all the molding machines. He also had to pay higher wages than in Chicago.

As a beginner, I had to look for the most economical situation. I could start my shop in an old, low-rent building in a neighborhood where plenty of good workers would accept the low wages suitable for the plastic molding industry.

Most industrial supply and service companies were still located in the city. We could get almost anything within a reasonable time in the city, while manufacturers in the suburbs had to wait. Furthermore, the water in the suburbs was hard and would need to be softened with salt. Water must be clean and soft for plastic molding, because chilled water is used in the molds to cool the plastic parts. Of course, water treatment would cost money, and salt-treated water did not taste good.

I decided to start my business in Chicago. I began to look at industrial building rentals in newspapers. When I had time, I drove along streets on the city's North Side, looking for "For Rent" signs. I spotted a small advertisement in the *Chicago Tribune*. A five-thousand-square-foot building was for rent for five hundred and fifty per month.

I said to myself, "It must be a very junky building for that price," but called the telephone number right away. The landlord said he would be happy to show me the building the next morning.

I wanted to make sure no one would rent the place before me. "I would like to see it tonight," I said, "say, within one hour. Is that all right?"

He was ready to go home, but agreed to wait for me.

The building was a garage with skylights and had been occupied by a wallpaper manufacturer. The company had manufactured felt wallpapers in a variety of colors by blowing the felt material onto glue-covered papers. During this process, the fuzzy felt flew all over the plant, covering everything, the beams, the joists, the windowsills, the electrical wires. It filled the grooves between bricks, the cracks in the cement floor, and the electric outlet boxes. Paper scraps, paperboards, and pieces of lumber lay scattered all over the floor. The lighting was so poor, I couldn't see very much.

"This building is lucky," the landlord told me. "Every tenant has been successful, expanded, and moved to a larger plant."

I said to myself, "Good luck, good labor, good water, that's enough for me." Five thousand square feet was the right size, and five hundred and fifty per month a good price. The building was warm even in winter. Although it needed a lot of cleaning, I decided to take it. I gave the landlord one thousand one hundred dollars for a two-month deposit and could take occupancy the first day of 1969.

In the middle of December 1968, three days before I planned to give notice, The Talker called me to his office and told me he didn't need my services anymore. I told him I would go out to lunch and not come back.

"You can stay two more weeks, you know," he reminded me.

"Thank you, but no," I said.

I felt neither victorious nor defeated. The entire episode in the molding shop disappeared from my mind quickly as June and I prepared to open our business the first thing in the New Year. My thoughts were only on the business.

On January 2, 1969, at eight o'clock, June and I arrived at the building to open our shop. The moment we walked in the front door, we realized the temperature inside the building was about the same as outside.

"Wow, it's cold!" I yelled.

In Chicago, the coldest time is around New Year's Day, and that year was no exception. Snow covered the sidewalk in the front, and when we opened up the garage door in the rear, the whole area outside was all snow-covered ice and very bumpy.

Sure enough, the boiler had blown out. I called the landlord immediately and he promised to come, but he didn't show up until the afternoon. He examined the boiler and called his heating man to come fix it. I also called the Chicago Water Department; the water pipes were frozen, and it was their responsibility to fix them.

By about two o'clock in the afternoon, the boiler man and the Water Department men arrived at the rear door. As June tried to step out of the way, she slipped and fell on the ice. Fortunately, her very heavy jacket cushioned her, and she was not hurt. By eight o'clock that evening, the boiler got started and the pipes thawed out. Everyone went home without saying goodbye. The workmen were all exhausted, and June and I were dog-tired.

Cleaning up a felt-covered building was not as easy as we had thought. Getting the floor in shape wasn't too difficult, but cleaning the ceiling turned out to be a dangerous job. We had to use tall ladders, long-handled brooms, and an industrial vacuum.

Wally, my investor friend from the plastic molding shop, told me that his son in college could use a part-time job helping me clean up the place. He was a very nice boy, and I was happy to hire him. It took us a whole week to clean up the building. Only then was I able to think about the layout. I was tempted to paint the walls, but good sense stopped me. I realized we should not spend money on things of secondary importance.

Furnishing the office was simple. The previous tenant had left behind two large wooden desks and two wooden chairs. The desks had scratched tops and wouldn't win a beauty contest, but they and the chairs were usable. One safe had been too heavy to move. I paid some money for it. I also brought from home an old blue sofa bed, and a used pink dinette set.

> **Confucius said: "One who feels no shame in wearing a shabby old gown while standing next to someone wearing fox and badger is without envy or greed. How can he not be good?"**

I had been asking friends to recommend a foreman for some time, but nobody could come up with the right one. After the power line and the molding machine were installed, just in time, Wally thought of a man working as an assistant foreman for a large molding company. According to Wally, this man was honest, hard working, and a good mechanic.

I interviewed Daniel Szajowski and hired him as foreman, my first and only employee. Wally must have done some fancy talking to get such a conservative person to take such a big chance with me.

Our first task was to get our plant set up and equipped for production. We very carefully set our priorities. For instance, a platform hand truck had the highest priority because we would need it for loading or moving everything else.

We had to buy everything from scratch, and I had to pay cash for every purchase, because our new company had no credit. I laid my big checkbook on the front passenger seat of my compact white Chevelle and drove around for supplies while my foreman sat at the dinette table, drinking coffee and waiting for my telephone call. After I purchased something, I would give the supplier a check on the spot and then telephone Daniel and tell him what I'd bought and when it would be delivered, if the item was too large to be carried in my car.

To sit in a practically empty five-thousand-square-foot, high-ceilinged garage was not only lonesome, but spooky, particularly when the wind howled. The skylights made all kinds of noises: squeaking, slapping, banging, and knocking. When Daniel expected a delivery, he had to concentrate on listening for the doorbell. If the article to be delivered was too large for one man to handle, I went to help. In the meantime, I would catch up with my telephone calls.

Soon, we were all ready, and I began to look for business. As a beginner, I had no mold repair facilities, and no quality control procedures, so large corporations would not deal with us. The only way to get started would be to get overflow jobs from other custom molders who had too much to handle. This was called: "subcontracting." I had not dared to tell the man at the government agency the truth of the situation. He probably would not have understood and might have rejected our loan guarantee application.

Sunzi wrote in his *Art of War:* "Compare and know your strength and deficiency."

In the beginning, I didn't ask for favors from friends at big corporations. I only looked for subcontract jobs. Thus, I was not in want for things I did not deserve, which gave me a healthy mind.

My first call was to an old friend of mine, Dick Hansel. He was a working partner in a small, five-year-old plastic custom molding shop in a western suburb. I told him that we were up and running and would be happy to do some molding for him if he had any extra work. In a couple of days, he called back to say he had a short-run job he would like us to do.

This is a pleasant start, I thought with delight.

The next day, Dick Hansel's driver brought in a mold and some plastic resin. Dan set up the mold in the molding machine, and had the plastic resin heated in the oven. Then he said, "John, we need a machine operator."

"Now?" I asked. I thought he himself would run the machine.

"Well, yes, in a couple of hours," he answered casually.

The only thing left for me to do was to find a machine operator quickly. I walked to the corner snack shop where I had lunch every day and asked the proprietor if she knew anybody who wanted to work. She recommended a woman of about fifty-five. She spoke broken English and was a neat person of seemingly mild disposition. I asked her to report to work at our shop at noon.

She came on time. Dan gave her a cup of coffee and asked her to sit down and wait. He had trouble with the mold and finally reached the conclusion that the mold needed repair. By two o'clock, we let the woman go and paid her for two hours. So much for our auspicious beginning!

I called Dick Hansel and told him about the problem with the mold.

"I am sorry, John," he said. "We never tried that mold. In fact, we never even opened it up to look at it. I'll send the driver to pick it up with the resin."

Dick Hansel was an honest man. During the next month, he let us do quite a few short-run jobs.

In the meantime, we began to receive subcontracted work from other molders. My sales pitch started like this: "I am new in business." That meant I had no experience with the tricks of the trade, so I could be taken advantage of, to some degree. The next pitch was, "We do good work, and we have a brand new molding machine." Most of the small custom molders had old machines that didn't do as good a job as new ones.

The most important point, of course, was the price. I would say, "We are very cheap, as we need work badly. We do not have regular customers yet." This made established molders eager to start a relationship with me; they wanted a hungry molder with low prices.

Overflow jobs usually were urgent. Otherwise, the molder would simply wait and mold the parts later, when their shop was not so busy. In order to meet these urgent demands, I bought two more used molding machines. They served the purpose, but to get enough jobs to keep three machines running and our four employees, in addition to myself, busy, was quite difficult.

One Monday morning, while driving to work, I asked myself, "Where can I get more work?" I was all too aware that all three machines would be out of work within a day or two. Trying hard to figure out what to do, I shook and perspired. I hadn't realized I was so vulnerable, sensitive, and weak.

I walked from the back door straight to my office near the front entrance without looking at the machines or my employees. The moment I sat down in my chair, Dan stuck his head inside my office door.

"John, we'll be out of work by tomorrow."

"I know," I answered. I grabbed the industrial yellow pages telephone book, found the molders page, and began to call all of them, starting from the letter *A*, to ask for subcontracted jobs. Nineteen-sixty-nine was not a good year for custom molders; molding jobs were scarce. I didn't get a positive answer until I reached the letter *K*.

"Well, I may have something for you," Mr. Kirkpatrick said. "Why don't you come and take a look?"

The company was in Indiana, and I drove nearly an hour before I found the place. The man had a fairly successful custom molding shop, and I was impressed with his office, which was paneled with knotty pine. Mr. Kirkpatrick sat in a high-backed executive chair behind an expensive wooden desk. Soft music from two wall-hung stereo speakers muffled the noise of the plant.

"John, give me a price for these parts," he said, and then told me the weights of the parts and the cycle time I needed to calculate the price. Cycle time is the time in seconds it takes for the machine to complete a production cycle.

I added up the numbers, feeling a little nervous doing the calculations in front of the customer.

I got the jobs. Mr. Kirkpatrick's foreman loaded two small molds in the trunk of my car and hefted six bags of plastic resin onto the back seat. These jobs kept two machines busy for three days.

After we completed the jobs, Dan and I packed the twenty-five small cartons of finished parts into my two-door Chevelle. We squeezed every carton possible into the trunk and onto the back and front seats and the floors. The cartons blocked all the windows except the front windshield on the driver's side and the left side-mirror. I had tucked the invoice into my pocket, to deliver along with the merchandise. I received payment within a few days.

I thought this job would establish a good relationship with this company, but the unexpected happened: Mr. Kirkpatrick's foreman told me he had accepted all my parts in spite of some with molding defects. He hadn't reported this to the boss because he wanted to help me. Then he hinted I should treat him to dinner or at least lunch.

I knew my employees hadn't produced anything worse than what this man's shop produced themselves. If we had, then it was the foreman's responsibility to report the defects to his employer. I could never work with a man who expected bribes or free meals in exchange for future work, a man I could not respect. No matter what I might say, Mr. Kirkpatrick would never take my word over that of his foreman. And the foreman should have known that anyone who looked for subcontracting work did not have extra time and money for entertainment.

Chinese proverb: "To get along with a gentleman is easy; to work with a petty person is hard."

I looked at the foreman in disgust and left. I did not say thank you and never went back. On my way home, I tried to justify my breaking away from this company. I consoled myself with the thought that I hadn't lost much by writing them off. The drive between their facility and mine was too far, and the jobs were probably all short-runs.

That was not the only work I chose to give up. A toy company that specialized in plastic car and airplane models was located in a northern suburb. Its own molding plant took care of long run and trouble-free components; it outsourced the short-run jobs to small, alley molding shops. The company furnished the molds, resins, packing materials, and cycle time, but most of their cycle times were too fast for the old machines. As a result, most of the alley shops lost money doing their work. The toy makers knew they were cutting the throats of small guys, but got away with it, because alley shops were always hungry. I knew of an alley shop whose two partners did a lot of work for this model company and eventually went broke.

One time, I became so hungry that I took on a job from this model company. Well, everyone took a bath with them at least once; why not me? I put my best machine operator on the job, but still could not achieve the specified cycle time. I gave up after two days, having lost money on every part we made for them. When the production manager of the model company later called me to do more molding for them, I politely turned them down.

On another occasion, I obtained a subcontract job from an established molding company through a friend. The founder had retired, and his brother had taken over the business. The brother sent me a large mold and resins. Since we did not have tool facilities to examine the mold, we set it up in the machine, then noticed the mold had been badly damaged.

If I had been more experienced, I would have called the brother immediately and asked him to come examine the mold. Instead, my foreman, who had no business sense, tried to mold anyway, which made the whole mold look even worse.

I told the brother by phone what had happened, but he jumped into the conclusion that we'd smashed his mold. Furious, he sent people to collect the mold and resins the next day.

After a few days, when everybody had cooled off, I suggested he ask his foreman if the mold had been cleaned after the previous production run, and in what condition the mold had been.

His foreman told him that the mold had been cleaned and was in good shape. I knew right away this company had an unreliable and dishonest foreman who hid things from the boss, and that the company would be in trouble for sure before long. Because the brother didn't want to talk to me, I could not help him by telling him about his real problem. For several years, he and I never met or spoke to each other. Later, I heard he sank deeper and deeper into trouble until he was forced to sell the business dirt cheap.

About six months after I started my business, my friend Dick Hansel asked me to do him a favor. Their old plant had been located in a run-down town west of the city. Well-to-do people had moved away, and then the industries and businesses had left. Buildings were old, poverty took over the town, and crime followed. Their molding plant had been in an old brick building with steel doors, steel window guards, and other security measures. But one Saturday night burglars broke through the brick wall and vandalized the whole facility.

The owner and my friend had bought a building and made plans to move to the western suburb, but because of the severe damage caused by the vandals, management decided to proceed immediately, even before the electricity and a water system were in.

"We won't be back in production for another three months," he said. "In the meantime, can you do some molding for us? I'll have my driver deliver the molds and resins to you, and he'll pick up the production maybe a couple of times a week."

"Dick, this is a favor to me, not a favor to you," I said. "I need work. We'll do the best job we can for you."

As it turned out, Dick's company could not handle all their business for almost six months. This created a good opportunity for me. I believe that two factors made it possible. First, I was prepared and ready to do the job. Second, Dick Hansel thought of me as a trustworthy man; otherwise, he would have given the jobs to somebody else.

Chinese proverb: "Spider works hard spinning cobweb; flying insects will come."

Subcontract jobs could only make a very low profit. Usually I could earn no more than ten percent gross profit. Somebody else had obtained the job, and naturally, he deserved more profit, even if he did not produce the products. Therefore, although I had been able to keep my machines fairly busy, my cash flow was quite poor.

Under such financial conditions, I did not want to spend money to buy a tumbler for coloring plastic resins. Instead, we would put one hundred pounds of natural resin into a paper drum, add the right amount of colorant to the resin, close and seal the drum, and lay the drum down sideways on the floor. Dan would push, rolling the drum toward me from about fifteen feet away, and I then rolled the drum back to him. After several rounds of rolling back and forth, the color was mixed surprisingly well. Unfortunately, this process ate into my valuable time and sometimes got my clothes dirty. I liked to be at least clean when I received visitors, particularly customers. Nevertheless, coloring resins was not a serious concern.

A much bigger problem was people: Machine operators often did not show up for work. If one operator did not report to work, a machine had to be shut down. Such a loss of production meant a reduction of revenue, and thus decreased profit.

What could I do? I tried to call the missing employees, but most of these workers had no telephone. Often I would drive to their homes to see if I could pick them up and bring them to our plant. Usually, when I rang the doorbell, the girl would come down the stairs apologizing for being late. I'd give her a ride to work.

One time, a lady did not show up, and though I had never been to her place before, I decided to see if I could find her. I found her address in a deteriorating neighborhood and rang the doorbell. Nobody answered. I rang again, and she came to the top of the stairway in pajamas with the top two buttons opened. Her hair was tousled and she was barefoot. Behind her stood two teenage girls dressed in bras and bikini underpants. They just looked at me curiously.

"You want to come to work?" I asked.

She smiled and answered, "You want to come up?"

Something about the situation seemed unsavory. "If you want to come to work, come as soon as you can," I told her, and hurried from the building.

After this incident, I stopped picking up workers.

On the other end of the spectrum, my insurance man wanted to come and see me often. He treated me like a youngster, although he was only a middle-aged man. Although my insurance policy was small, he invited me to lunch. Normally, I didn't go to lunch with service people or suppliers, because I didn't have the time. But this time I said yes.

The man drove me to a delicatessen, where it was so noisy that I could not hear clearly what he said. He was well groomed and smelled mildly of cologne. To show his success, he wore a short mink coat in the early spring. After the lunch, he took me back to my office. On the way, he showed me how luxurious his Cadillac was. He played cassette music just to demonstrate how enjoyable it could be.

"When you are successful, you will be riding like this," he said.

I thanked him, but wished I'd never gone.

Soon, he called me again for lunch, and I told him I couldn't go with anyone except my customers, because I had no free time. If he had no business to talk about, I asked him not call me. I hope he understood how precious my time was, and that I didn't mean to be rude.

In the beginning, June helped a great deal in the office. She answered telephones, did the payroll, typed letters, and so on. She also cleaned the office and the washroom.

Later, I hired a part-time secretary, a personal friend of a nice couple who worked for us in the factory. She came in only three mornings a week, and this arrangement suited both of us. She could type a little, but basically was a neighborhood housewife. She answered the telephone in such a not businesslike manner, I often thought she was talking to her next-door neighbor. During my absence, I knew she chatted away on the phone just as if she were home in her own kitchen making spaghetti sauce.

June came to the office occasionally, and I could always count on her. If I had a problem and could not make up my mind about what to do, I always discussed it with her, and often she could open up other options. I had to be very careful to remember she was my wife, not my secretary, and not to take her help for granted.

One time, she asked me, "How come you are so charming when a lady visitor is here?"

Her observation might have been true, but she neglected to notice I also tried to be charming with male visitors, particularly when the visitor was a customer! I explained this to her, but she was not completely convinced.

Before long, my part-time secretary quit because her kids needed her at home. I hired another young lady named Mary, a lovely person. She had fair complexion and was a little plump.

Normally, a secretary would not be crabby with me, but one day Mary seemed extremely sensitive. She did not talk much and had no smile. She snapped her ballpoint pen on her desk continuously, making a clicking sound that began to drive me crazy.

I walked over to her desk. "Mary, what is bothering you?"

Without looking up at me, she said, "Nothing. Why?"

"Do you feel okay?" I asked in a low voice.

She appeared insulted and answered, "Of course I feel okay."

"Mary, you go home now," I told her, "and come to work the day after tomorrow when you feel better. You will be paid as usual."

She left the office a few hours early. I never did find out what was bugging her, but when she came back a couple of days later, everything was fine.

Confucius said: "If the superior cherishes understanding and courtesy, people will not be disrespectful."

After a few months in business, I was short on time and cash. At this crucial period, I received a letter from the investor who was my former boss. He said one of his best friends from Switzerland wanted to buy a house, but did not have enough money for a down payment. He wondered if he could withdraw his investment with me so he could loan the money to his friend.

Confucius said: "we must practice five attitudes to be considered benevolent: respect, tolerance, trustworthiness, diligence, and generosity.

This man had put up his savings to invest in my venture, because he trusted me. Now, for whatever reason, he had changed his mind. I could not fail him. Wishing to prove my own trustworthiness, I mailed him a check for his total investment, plus interest.

When I told him I had already sent him the check, he thanked me. At that time, he didn't know that I'd paid him interest at the rate I would have paid a bank. He knew I didn't have to pay him interest, because that money was ownership investment. I was not a saint; I simply wanted to give my friend a fair deal, and to make him a happy and loyal friend. I hoped he would tell others how fair I'd been, and consequently, I would build a reputation.

I had to be willing to accept a minimal tangible loss in order to gain much more intangibly. Because of this investment withdrawal, I had to go to the bank several times to get short-term loans to meet payrolls. I called my investors, asking them if they had extra money to invest more in our company, as we were badly short of cash. The only one who sent more money was my best friend, Joe Wang, who was not a rich man. He was motivated by a desire to help, not to get rich. At that time, his elder son was ill.

Wally, the investor from the molding shop, had put up all his savings with me already and could not invest any more. I believed that he would have, if he could, because he still often helped me technically, when I needed it.

My last telephone call was to Mr. Fu. I asked him if he would invest more money in our company.

In a charming and loving voice, he said politely, "Ah, no, oh no more."

I could imagine a well-mannered smile on his face. I knew then, that he had decided to limit his investment to a definite amount no matter what. His only hobby was gambling, and he played blackjack and poker well. His investment with me was like playing a game of poker, limiting his loss. He never gave a thought that if I was seriously in trouble, my venture might fail entirely.

I felt that if he had considered himself a friend, he should have helped me to avoid another failure, since he could easily do it without risking much. Now, I had no doubt about where we stood with each other and, therefore, didn't feel sorry for myself anymore. I was, in a way, beginning to feel grateful that he did not invest more, because I would have hated to see him reaping so much profit in the future.

5

Getting My Own Customers

"You can't catch a cub without going into the tiger's den."

—Chinese proverb

"My name is Larry Abrams," the voice at the other end of the phone said. "I'd like you to quote me on a couple of plastic items. Can I meet you and see your plant?"

"Of course," I answered, pleasantly surprised. So far I had only been able to attract low-profit subcontracting work. "When do you want to come?"

"How about right now?"

Ten minutes later, he arrived: a big, nice-looking fellow who gave the impression of being smart. His suit was clean, but not expensive in cut or fabric.

I showed him my three molding machines, one of which was new, and some plastic parts we had molded. I was sure he had noticed I had no secretary and no new furniture. He could easily deduce that we had very low overhead and knew how to mold.

During our conversation, I told Mr. Abrams I was Chinese and college educated, and he probably figured I was naive about the rough-and-tough plastic molding business. From his face, I could see he was pleased and saying to himself, "I can get a real bargain here."

"I am a salesman," he told me. "I know many companies that need molded plastic parts. I get orders from them and have molders to make the parts for me. I deliver the production to the customers." He paused and continued, "I also have a factory doing second operations for the customers."

"I see," I thought, "Mr. Abrams is actually a molding broker." He went out to his car and brought back two plastic parts, handed them to me, and asked for a quote, adding, "The prices have to be very low."

Before even glancing at the parts, I said, "You can see my overhead is low. My normal profit margin is fifteen percent. For you, I will make it ten percent. I have to make some money." Actually, I wished I could get fifteen percent profit on jobs I would receive directly from my own customers. So far, I'd had no direct customers.

After we agreed on prices for the two parts, Mr. Abrams left. Two days later, he brought me two molds and resins. After that, he gave me more business, and he would drop in from time to time just to see how we were doing.

Before long, I received another phone call from a prospect, a Mr. Giles, who said he had a plastic part he wanted me to mold. "Could you come to see me?" he asked.

"Yes. When?"

"How about right now?"

This sounded familiar, and I went right away. Mr. Giles had a small factory that made plastic displays and advertising items. He had a Semitic-looking face, and I guessed he was Jewish and might just know Larry Abrams. I decide to give Mr. Abrams's name as a reference, since this Mr. Giles had not seen my plant.

"You can ask him," I said. "He'll tell you what he thinks about us."

It turned out Mr. Giles and Mr. Abrams knew each other very well. "Larry has a couple of girls doing some second operation work," he told me, laughing. "They work while he's in his factory watching them, but they stop working as soon as he goes out."

I thought to myself, "He can't make money this way."

Eventually, I got the job from Mr. Giles. From these two gentlemen I learned that many small businesses needed modest quantities of various plastic products or components. The owners could not afford to buy from the large, sophisticated molding companies, partially because their volume was relatively insignificant. They, therefore, were constantly searching for newcomers who were small, hungry, and able to mold. I had not known how to find such customers, because they were spread over all industries, but through word-of-mouth, they began to find me.

Soon, I was making musical bells, key chains, ornaments, and other novelties for the premium people. I cut my prices to the bone, but these businessmen helped me phase out subcontracts and build up my own clientele.

I was interested to observe that the premium makers were all Jewish, just like years earlier, when all the hand-laundry shops were owned by Chinese, even the one in New York called the "Pat Murphy Chinese Hand Laundry." The story went like this: When a Chinese fellow came to the U.S., he lined up behind a tall

Irishman at the immigration window. When he got to the window, the officer asked, "What's your name?" He answered, "Sam Sing." The officer thought he said "same thing", so he wrote his name as Pat Murphy.

At the time, I was molding for the premium makers, discrimination against Chinese and Jews had lessened, but they were still regarded as different from whites. True or false, I gained the impression that Jewish people generally liked doing business with Chinese.

One day, I received an inquiry by mail from a Mr. Hirsh, owner of a premium company, requesting a quotation for a plastic button.

In those days, although competition among molders was intense, companies that used plastic components did not have too much competition for their products from abroad and usually could absorb a higher cost of components without hurting their sales. Thus, molders normally could tag on a twenty-percent gross profit over the calculated cost. I sent out many quotations with a twenty-percent markup, and did so on the button.

After about a week, Mr. Hirsh called and said he would like to do business with me. A mutual friend had told him about our quality work. But he said my price was too high.

I told him I would look my quotation over and call him back. I figured that he would not have called me if my price weren't in line. It might even be the lowest quote he received, but he would still want it lower, if possible.

I knew Mr. Hirsh would not allow me the twenty-percent going rate. I made a new quotation sheet in which I increased the estimated production cycle time, thus increased my cost, and by reducing my markup from twenty percent to ten percent, the price remained about the same. Then I called him and invited him to come and see our factory, and to discuss the price for the button.

He came the next day and sat on the old but clean blue sofa. Our desks and chairs were also old but clean. Our factory was always orderly. Although we had only three machines and three operators, everyone was full of spirit and concentrating on the work.

Then, we walked back to my office and I invited him to sit in the chair opposite mine and look over my quotation sheet.

"As you can see, our place is an efficient, quality plant," I told him. "Since I am new, I do not have many customers and am eager to please. If you can find any item that can be reduced, let's discuss it. But you have to let me make some money."

Mr. Hirsh knew something about molding but not enough to bluff me. "The cycle time seems too high," he said.

I told him the button was quite heavy and needed longer molding time. Before he left, he gave me an order for the button at my price. He became a regular customer, giving me small jobs from time to time.

In the meantime, Mr. Abrams, the molding broker, had given me more business, primarily for two vending machine manufacturers. The molds he had built for them were very poorly constructed. The quality of the products made with these molds was substandard, often with defects. Every time there was a problem with a product, he would meet with the customer and always found a way for the customer to use the defective parts. No money was provided for mold maintenance, so the supplier, molding broker, and customer all faced the reality of compromised quality.

After about a year, Larry Abrams walked into my office and, without hesitation, asked, "Would you like to buy me out?"

I was surprised. "Why do you want to sell?"

"Because I'm not making money," he answered flatly, pacing nervously. "It's too much work for me, and it is not worth it."

I made my decision right away. "I'd like to buy you out."

He showed me a long list of molds and customers. Without seeing the molds, I knew they were junk, but the customers were not fussy about the quality of their products. Mr. Abrams wanted a certain amount of cash, and I didn't argue. He offered to be my sales manager, earning a five percent commission on sales through him without salary, and I agreed.

Just at the moment, I was dealing with Larry, I received a phone call from Mr. Miller, the counselor assigned to me as an advisor by the government agency that guaranteed my bank loan. He was a retired businessman who volunteered at the agency to help small businesses. He had had a molding company of his own years before and had sold his business when he retired.

I told him I was buying Abrams out.

"What are the terms?" he asked. Before I could tell him, he continued, "You know, Larry Abrams is a smart cookie. I know him well."

When I explained I would pay so much cash up front, and hire Abrams as sales manager on five-percent commission, he objected sharply.

"No! That's too much! You can't pay him that much up front and still give him a job on commission!" Quite excited, Mr. Miller continued. "Abrams wants to sell, so he must be desperate. If he says he is not making money, he must be losing money. I suggest you hold him off, and you can buy his business with very little cash."

"Mr. Miller, no deal is a good deal if it is not fair to both parties," I said. "I believe what I'm going to pay for his business is a bargain to me. You see, among his long list of customers, two of them are medium-sized companies, and I could get a lot of business from them. It would be impossible for me to knock on doors and land two direct customers like those. That's worth two years of my time, if not longer. I want those two customers, and I think I should pay for them."

"But if you can get them cheaper, why not?" he argued.

This was, and still is, the basic concept of most business people I knew, but has never been my way.

Chinese proverb: "Insatiable greed will lose."

"If I hold off, how much can I save?" I said. "For a small amount of money, I would be taking a big risk of losing the deal. If he sells to somebody else, when will I get another opportunity to secure two large customers of my own?"

"Oh, nobody would want that junk business," Miller scoffed.

"You might be right. But I don't want to take that chance," I explained. "For the time I hold off the deal, I could start making money by doing business with these customers directly."

Mr. Miller still wasn't convinced. He didn't like the deal, but showed no anger toward me.

When I negotiated the contract with Mr. Abrams, he wanted five years' employment. I insisted on two, and he went along. I guessed he figured the contract would be renewed anyway. He thought highly of himself and believed I would need him forever.

I didn't bother to engage a lawyer for this contract. I thought it was simple enough, and of course, I wanted to save every penny I could. He had a lawyer, though, a personal friend of his. This lawyer knocked me around left and right, nibbling at word after word.

The contract finally was signed, and Mr. Abrams became our sales manager. He was very happy and cooperative. I let him take one of the two old wooden desks and chairs. He came in every morning, made some phone calls, and visited some customers. When we had a quality problem, he usually went to the customer and ironed it out.

For instance, we were molding a clear Lexan cover plate for a Coca-Cola vending machine. It had to be strong enough to withstand vandalism. For one shipment, the customer complained that the plate cracked during a hammer test.

Larry and I went to the customer's plant to see the quality control man. He showed us the cracked plate. Larry took a few plates from the carton and hit them near the edge with the rubber mallet. The plates deformed and bent, but did not crack. The quality control man had hit the plates at dead center, causing them to deform and crack.

Mr. Abrams and I went to the office to show the buyer the deformed plates.

"The hammer test wasn't fair," Mr. Abrams said. "A juvenile could hardly have such a large mallet and hit the plate in the center with such a powerful blow. A strong adult would not crack the plate to steal some coins."

The buyer looked at the plates, showed them to his boss, and told us they would hammer-test some more. If none cracked, they would accept the lot.

Actually, the plates were substandard, or at least borderline. Had they been molded correctly, a mallet never would have cracked them. It saved us a lot of extra work and money that the customer finally accepted the lot, but the situation gnawed at me.

Not long thereafter, Mr. Abrams intervened again on our behalf with a Canadian firm for which we made a decorative plated part. During one run, the color was a little off. I asked him if we should show a sample to the customer and make sure it was acceptable before we made the shipment. He said if we asked, most likely they would reject the parts, because he knew at the time, the customer was not in urgent need of them. But since only a small batch of parts were not the correct color, Mr. Abrams suggested we mix a few of the off-colored ones in each of the cartons of the correct ones.

"They'll never find them," he said.

This was not only dishonest, but also dangerous, because if I cheated even once and was caught, I would certainly lose one customer and possibly many others.

We were such a small company that every penny counted, so I went along with him, even though it compromised my principles. I regretted the decision, however. To stay absolutely honest at all times is good business; a good reputation is invaluable. Building a trustworthy reputation requires constant effort, and maintaining the reputation requires tireless discipline.

These experiences with Abrams bothered me a great deal. From that time on, whenever he suggested something that violated my moral code, I refused to follow his suggestions.

Confucius said: "Do not impose on others what you yourself do not want."

The other vending machine manufacturer I acquired as a customer from Mr. Abrams was a far cry from the one for whom we made the plates. This company was poorly managed, and the executives had changed two or three times since we began doing business with them. Often they could not pay their bills, and in a few months, they owed us eighteen thousand dollars, a large sum for a small company like us.

I called their accounting department. The person was new and transferred me to another man. This man said they would pay me right away, but after a week no check had come. I called the buyer again, who said he would talk to his boss, but nothing happened.

After a few more weeks, I made my final call and said, "Mr. Buyer, there will be no shipment to you until you pay up the existing invoices. Next time when you place an order, please send a check with the order, otherwise I will not make the parts for you."

Apparently, he didn't pay much attention to what I had said, for within a month he called, wanting some parts. Again, I told him to send a check to pay for the existing invoices and another check for the new order.

"You can't do that," he objected loudly.

"Yes, I can," I said.

He hung up on me.

After another three weeks, he called again and said, "John, I'll send the check to pay all the bills. You make a shipment of the new order as soon as you can."

"I can't do that," I said. "You have to send another check for the full payment of the new order."

He became very angry and hung up on me again.

Two weeks later, he called back and asked, "John, do you have inventory of the parts I ordered?"

"No, I don't," I said.

"How long will it take to make them for me?" he asked in a friendly voice.

"I can do it immediately," I answered, "and I can make partial shipment the day after tomorrow if you need them. Otherwise, I'd need a week, as the quantity is not large."

That afternoon he sent a man to our office with two checks, one for the eighteen thousand dollars they'd owed us for many months and the other for the new order. We produced and delivered the parts to them within a week.

Then I called the buyer and asked him to find another supplier, as we did not wish to do business with them anymore. To have a customer like that was not good business. It wasted too much time and created a bad environment.

This vending machine manufacturer was not the only company in bad shape and unable pay bills. Others intentionally paid as late as possible, forty-five days or even sixty days after the invoice date, in order to use suppliers' money as their working capital.

I have always believed that any good company should make money through their business operations, and not by cheating suppliers. I believed they would lose in some other aspects.

We normally paid within thirty days without delay. If a customer offered a one-or two-percent ten-day discount, we paid in ten days and took the discount. We never gave a discount, because many companies paid late but still took the discount.

We always paid service people, such as contractors, consultants, engineers, electricians, repairmen, and so forth, as soon as we received their invoices. The next time, we needed them, they would do our job promptly. When we had emergency work, they would come right away, sometimes even getting off an ongoing job. The amount of payment for personal services was usually relatively small. To us, paying right away or paying a month later meant very little difference financially, so why not show our appreciation for their work? This way, everybody was happy, and our reward was good service. Nothing speaks louder than immediately paid checks.

Chinese proverb: "With money, you can make a ghost push the mill."

Early in 1970, one year after we opened our doors, a tall man suddenly walked into my office and introduced himself as Jim Adams, the procurement supervisor of the Kentucky plant of IBM Corporation. He asked for a tour of our factory, and I showed him the building, the three molding machines, and some resins stored at one corner with the platform hand truck.

Although we had cleaned out all the felt left over by the wallpaper manufacturer, the brick walls were dark and damaged at places. The skylights were still making noises. I was sure Mr. Adams noticed the pink dinette set and coffee pot on it. He thanked me for the tour and disappeared through the narrow door into the city street. I wondered what he was trying to accomplish, and whether he would come back again. He'd left so quickly, I'd failed to get his business card.

I had little time to worry about this, however. My friend Edward, a plastic product designer, had designed a line of respiratory apparatus for a newly organized firm, and had recommended me as a possible supplier. The firm's founder was a lawyer named Paul O'Brien who knew nothing about plastics or respiratory medicine. The established plastic molders refused to quote on his products, because his firm had not established credit, and the founder was novice in the business he'd entered. The establishment must also have thought O'Brien's apparatus would be complicated and difficult to mold.

Mr. O'Brien, not knowing how to qualify a molder, relied on his trust in the designer. He thought our prices were good. Apparently Edward had given him some idea as to how much these products should cost. Thus we received a contract for the whole line of their products.

The products were very complicated to mold, and we had all kinds of trouble. I thought some of the designs could be simplified, but I didn't dare make that suggestion, because Edward had recommended us for the business. We tried hard and did the best we could on all the items.

One day, we were ready to try out a new mold of a very complex construction. Normally, we did not expect a satisfactory product on the first trial. Mr. O'Brien was market-minded, however, and he had told hospitals some time previously that they could expect samples at around the time of the mold trial.

He and his new president, Walt Martin, came to watch the trial and wait for samples. I had also asked the mold maker and mold designer to come lend a hand. I told the customers that making samples for hospitals would be impossible at the first trial, but Mr. O'Brien and Mr. Martin insisted.

The situation became very serious. The mold was not set up until five o'clock. I invited the executives to a small tavern half a block away from our plant. We sat at a tiny table to sip beer and nibble on fried shrimp. The mold designer acted as a messenger, walking back and forth between the factory and the tavern. Since nothing of importance was happening, he would just stroll to the tavern every fifteen minutes or so to report to us that no samples had been produced yet.

At nine o'clock the mold jammed, and many hours would be needed to repair it. When the mold designer reported this bad news to us in the tavern, Mr. Martin yelled, "God damn it!"

Mr. O'Brien stood up and shouted, "Shit!"

"It is a very complicated mold," I said in a low voice. "We'll keep working and bring you samples as soon as we can. How about having something to eat before you leave?"

Both of them said no, and the men went home angry and disappointed. Later on, Edward simplified the product, and by the next spring, we were satisfactorily producing all the products they needed.

Two years later, while we continued to struggle with new respiratory equipment, the tall man from Kentucky, Jim Adams, showed up again. He said he had been visiting some companies in Chicago and had taken the opportunity to stop by and see how we were doing. I again gave him a tour, and he left without saying anything, just as before.

A few months later, we added two more used molding machines that were in fairly good shape and hired operators to run them, bringing our employees to six.

We also found a reliable mold shop that was only about fifteen minutes away from our plant. Its owners, the Sigler brothers, had done good work for us, and gradually we built a trusting relationship. Eventually, we made an agreement that we would let them do all of our mold making and repair work. In return, they would give our mold repairs first priority. Such an arrangement was like having our own tool shop.

Although we were making advancements, we still had to improve our quality-control procedures. We depended on our machine operators and foreman to inspect the production.

Larry Abrams had been with us almost two years, but he had not secured any new customers; he concentrated on solving small problems with existing customers. One day, our conversation provided me with an opportunity to speak openly to him.

"Larry," I said, "you are a very clever man. Why do you waste so much energy trying to gain a few hundred dollars here or avoid paying a few hundred dollars there? Why don't you go out and get some big jobs from large companies? The time and effort are the same."

"It's not that easy, John," he answered.

I didn't know if my conversation had any impact on his work, but a few weeks later he walked in one morning and said, "You owe me seventeen hundred dollars. That is five percent commission on the molds I sold."

What a shock! In the plastic industry, commission is paid only on products delivered and never on tooling or molds sold. He knew it, I knew it, and everybody else knew it.

"No commission on molds and tooling is the rule of the plastic industry," I countered.

"It's not stated in the contract," he argued.

"Maybe we didn't say so in the contract," I said, "but that's the commonly known practice. You would enforce the contract that way?"

"My lawyer said I should," he replied.

"Apparently you and your lawyer have just found this loophole in the contract." I looked him directly in the eyes and asked, "Are you sure for seventeen hundred dollars you would sell your honesty?"

"Well, seventeen hundred dollars is seventeen hundred dollars," he stated.

What a stupid, pitiful man! I took out my checkbook and wrote him a check for the full amount. "Here," I said. "For seventeen hundred dollars, I will not fight you in court."

Chinese proverb: "It is the greatest sorrow when the conscience is dead."

After this, he went about his business normally, as if nothing had happened. On the thirtieth day before his employment contract expired, I told him our contract would not be renewed.

"You mean I am fired?" he asked, surprised.

Both Larry and his lawyer should have known that no employer would keep a man who was cheating. People say it's a good thing to have a tough lawyer on your side. But this one, although very tough, certainly had not given Larry beneficial advice.

Confucius said: "A petty person cannot be given important responsibilities, but can be relied on for trivial assignments."

The best way for a person to be successful is to work harmoniously with people around him, to progress and grow together. If he treats everyone else like an adversary, he will soon have no allies. Larry's lawyer had advised him to treat his employer as an enemy and to win whatever he could. By following this counsel, Mr. Abrams won a battle but lost the war.

We had been producing a plastic button for Mr. Hirsh's premium company for over two years. One day, Mr. Hirsh called me and complained about defective buttons he could not use. He wanted me to come to his office right away to examine them.

I drove over half an hour to get there. Mr. Hirsh told me that I had to take back the defective buttons. Then he called his foreman in. The foreman said he had already used every button we had sent them. In spite of that, Mr. Hirsh insisted they had received defective buttons and told his foreman to go look for them.

"Just how many bad ones were there?" I asked.

"About ten percent," he grumbled. "Probably they've already been thrown away."

"You can't even show me one bad button!" I said. "As long as I'm here, could you pay me that invoice?"

"I don't mind paying you, but how about the ten percent rejects?" he replied.

I looked him in the eyes, but saw no shame. "In order to save time," I offered, "why not let me give you a ten percent discount, and you give me a check?"

Of course he agreed. Then I told him, "In the future, please don't ask me to drop everything to come to see you. It's not the money, it's the time. Today I wasted two hours for you."

He did not say anything. We shook hands and I left. But although only a small amount of money was involved, such behavior left a bad taste.

One day, I received a call from a Mr. von Besser, asking me to come to his office to see some plastic components he wanted me to quote on. His office was in the rundown area of Chicago's south side, and in a building where the whole block had practically been cleared out. No other buildings were nearby, and not many people were around, either.

Why would anybody want to have an office or plant at such a place? I wondered, pulling my car into his parking lot.

When I walked up stairs, however, I saw the offices were nicely arranged. Mr. von Besser, dressed in a blue business suit, sat regally behind a large desk, looking like a banker.

"Thank you for coming so quickly," he said. "Here are the components of our ski bindings, the mechanism to fasten the boot to the ski. I'd like you to quote for us in various quantities."

He seemed to be an intelligent and commanding businessman, and I was sure he had acquired a good number of quotations. I gave him a fair price and left.

Finally, he selected us, and we served him diligently year after year. He ran his business like a family business, with his wife actively participating. He acted like a tough boss, but when I got to know him, I found he was a very good hearted man.

Eventually, we became good friends, and so did our wives. Since the ski-binding business was in a mature industry, our friend had cash-flow problems and often paid us late. I never complained. Unfortunately, they had to close their business in Chicago and start a new venture in the South. I felt touched and grateful, when I learned that they tried very hard to pay all our bills before they filed for bankruptcy. I believe that our mutual respect and friendship influenced his decision.

The prompt collection of our payments was also a challenge with the respiratory apparatus company we had served since the early days of our business. Its customers were hospitals, which never paid on time, so we got paid late in turn. I knew Paul O'Brien and Walt Martin well, and we had become good friends, so I never worried about their paying our bills. Nevertheless, because Paul enjoyed good times and liked to show off, I often teased him about keeping his overhead low.

Actually, my jokes were built around a serious core. One day, I went to visit them and saw a big car in the boss's reserved parking space. When Paul and I walked by the parking area, he knew I'd noticed.

"I leased a big car," he explained, "because it costs only a few dollars more per month than a full sized car."

I laughed and assured him, "You can drive any car you wish, because your business is so successful."

Walt, the company president, held an MBA from Harvard. He always joked whenever he saw me. "John, are you keeping your overhead low?"

In fact, we did keep our overhead extremely low. After surviving for over three years, we still had the old sofa bed in my office for guests to sit on, and employees in the plant drank free coffee around the old pink dinette set that had only five pink chairs. As for me, I had traded my old Chevelle for a new medium-sized Montego. Due to these austerity measures, we had saved plenty of cash in the bank.

The assets I could count from my business were not just financial; I built up many personal assets in the way of friendships. During the years of my struggle for survival, I met many nice people. Some of them became my friends, and a few became good friends. The man who let me mold for him for nearly six months before his plant was ready treated me fairly and honestly. His family and mine often got together for dinner.

Another man, Mr. Olson, who owned a small molding shop on Chicago's south side, gave me many subcontract jobs during the early months of my business. When I had problems, he came over and helped me solve them. During his first visit to my shop, he even showed me how to seal a carton efficiently. I always remembered all the nice things he did, and said to myself, "Someday if he needs my help, I will do everything I can to repay him for his kindness."

In 1973 the world suffered an oil shortage. Because plastic resins are made from oil, we had a plastic resin shortage that created a crisis for plastic-products users as well as producers. Plastic molders suffered the most, particularly the small ones. Since the resin manufacturers could not supply the resins required by all the product manufacturers, they prioritized their major customers and crossed small users off their customer lists. They did reduce the supply to the large volume users as well, but that decreased their production only somewhat. Totally cutting off supplies to the small guys was a matter of life and death! Did they not have hearts?

I thought their decision to cater only to the large manufacturers was short-sighted. Some small companies might become big in the future. Furthermore, small businesses are important to the country's economy. Sadly, the government did not interfere with this unfair favoritism. I believed the resin suppliers should have reduced their shipments by an equal percentage to all customers.

I was fortunate; I had a decent salesman, Dick Stoutland, from one of our important resin suppliers. We used about five thousand pounds of polypropylene each month, and he gave us that much resin every month during the crisis.

"Dick, you do not know how much I appreciate your help," I told him. "I know our name was crossed off your list of customers. How can you manage to send us the resin every month?"

He said in a low voice, "John, don't mention it. When a guy receives a million pounds of resin a month, he doesn't know if he's five thousand pounds short, and that won't hurt him a bit."

I never forgot this man. I promised myself that when our business got established, I would find him and give him a special treat and certainly a reward. Years later, when we moved to our second building, I asked our customer service manager to locate him. Due to mergers among resin producers, nobody knew where he was, but I still hope I can find him some day.

Confucius said: "Repay benevolence with benevolence."

Not everyone was as lucky as I was during the oil shortage. My friend who had moved to the western suburb used a lot of polystyrene. They were really hurt when the resin supplier dropped them from the users' list and cut off the supply. He told me later that if the plastic shortage had lasted one more year, he would have been out of business. I saw this resin supplier as one of a pack of heartless animals. I vowed never to buy polystyrene from that company.

Since Jim Adams's second visit to our plant in 1972, our facilities had increased to five molding machines, and we had gained an affiliated tool shop. Although we still had no quality control system, we did produce complicated products as proof of our capability. As another year had passed, I gathered my courage, and telephoned him in Kentucky to invite him to visit us, when he next came to Chicago.

He referred me to one of his buyers. I contacted the buyer and described all the improvements and updates my business had enjoyed since Mr. Adams's first visit. After this conversation, I sent him some respiratory products to show him what we could do. They were quite impressed.

A few months later, this buyer came to Chicago and took the opportunity to check out our facilities. I drove him to the tool shop and introduced the Sigler brothers. He looked at everything, but said nothing.

Before he left, I asked him, "Why not just try us once?"

"I'll think about it," he said.

A few weeks after his departure, I telephoned and again asked him to give us a try. Before long, he sent me an inquiry, three years after Mr. Adams first came to see our place. Naturally, our price was very attractive, so we got the chance to show our capabilities, and in a few months we were in production.

IBM Corporation gradually became our most important customer, all thanks to the tall man from Kentucky.

6

Buying Own Plant

"**Dear may not be expensive, cheap may not be economical.**"

—**Chinese proverb**

When I first started out as a worker at The Talker's molding shop, the owner told me they always kept extra molding machines, so they could take on emergency jobs that otherwise would be lost. He wouldn't have given me this tip, if he had known I planned to start my own company, not that I would have adopted his policy as my own.

To me, any capacity not utilized means nonproductive investment, and idle machines are not good for the general morale. I like to see everything and everybody busy. My policy has always been to add a molding machine only when forced to do so by projected steady production demand. If one of our regular customers had a one-time urgent production need, we could always rearrange the production schedule or add Saturday hours to accommodate them.

After five years in business, we had five molding machines running and more business coming in. We lacked sufficient capacity to meet the consistent demand and needed more machines, but that meant we would need a larger plant. Since we had retained earnings, we decided to buy a building of our own. Meanwhile, we subcontracted the extra work to other molders. Of course, the first person we contacted to do our overflow work was my friend Mr. Olson, who had helped me when I started Magenta.

In the five years I had been in business, many people had moved to the suburbs, including working-class families. Now, I wondered if we should leave Chicago and move to the suburbs as well. The city had many disadvantages: real-estate taxes were high and security poor. Night or day, my employees were in danger of being robbed.

Even with the many drawbacks, I decided to stay in the city, but in a nice area, because in Chicago we had one important advantage over the suburbs: the prompt availability of temporary help. Companies in the suburbs had to notify temp agencies at least one day in advance, so the agency could line up the correct number of workers the next morning and deliver them in a van to the various plants. As for the night shift, getting replacements on short notice was out of the question.

In the city, if one operator didn't show up, we could call the temp agency at eight o'clock in the morning and have a replacement in less than an hour. We could place an order for a number of temporary workers for the night shift by as late as four or five o'clock in the afternoon. This meant no shutdown of molding machines for our continuous three-shift production. If the worker was inexperienced, we could always assign him or her to a simple job, and let our regular employees do the more difficult ones.

Sunzi wrote in his *Art of War*: "Having advantage to gain, advance; without advantage, stop."

To house a plastic-molding operation, a building had to have a strong floor, a high ceiling, good ventilation, and so on, but my main concern was location. We did not want to be near the subway or bus stations, because many undesirables traveled by train or bus, could walk to the office to ask for a handout or to loiter near the plant. Such a location encouraged burglary and vandalism. We also didn't want to be in a residential section, near a school or public park. With kids around, vandalism certainly would occur.

An industrial park would be safe, but I did not want to be in one. Large corporations in industrial parks paid relatively high wages, and we couldn't compete with them for workers. Many larger plants had unions. My employees were mostly unskilled workers, and the wages could not compare with the wages of skilled workers in a union shop. Therefore, I did not want to be where we would attract the attention of union organizers with unrealistic demands.

My goal was to find a larger building near our current location, so no employees would have to quit due to the move. Unfortunately, the area housed few large buildings, and we would need a building about five times larger than the rented one. That would serve us for roughly ten years before we would have to relocate again. In the city, we couldn't expect to find a building with an adjacent empty lot for future expansion, but I mentally added that feature to my list of ideal features. We would just have to start looking.

First I telephoned Mr. Miller, our counselor from the government agency, and told him I was ready to buy a building. I thought he might be able to help, since he dealt with industrial real estate.

"Where are you going to buy the building?" he asked.

"On the northwest side, near where we are," I answered.

He immediately suggested, "John, why don't you move to the suburbs? I can help you locate some real bargains. There are many new buildings of all sizes."

"We've decided to stay in Chicago," I answered.

Then he said in a very low voice, "I see. If you need any help, call me any time."

I thanked him, and he hung up. Of course a government agency volunteer had the privilege of trying to sell me one of his buildings in the suburbs. But as an advisor, I thought at least he should have offered to recommend an industrial real estate broker to locate a building in Chicago for me. I guess some people won't do anything for nothing.

Chinese proverb: "Do someone a favor, and actually you may have done yourself a favor."

I contacted several industrial real-estate brokers and told them what I was looking for. An immigrant from Germany, Sol Goldman, enthusiastically took me to see several industrial buildings over the course of a few months, but none came close to meeting our requirements.

One day, I saw a newspaper advertisement for an industrial building being sold by a private party. I called right away and went to look at the building. It was located at the corner of a commercial street by a residential street not far from our current plant. It had a small parking lot along the residential street. The neighborhood was fairly good, mixed with Poles, Germans, and Italians. The subway ran far away to the east, but the bus line passed by the front door. The expressway could be reached within minutes, and the airport was about half an hour away.

I found the location quite desirable, except the side door was on a residential street.

The interior was desirable as well. The building had twenty-four thousand square feet. One section was new and had a high ceiling. An area in the older section had several apartments on the second floor occupied by tenants.

When a man plans to sell his building by himself, he's trying to save the broker's commission. Such a man is more difficult to deal with than a broker. Not a good negotiator, I figured I would probably pay more if I dealt directly with the seller rather than using my broker, even if I had to pay the broker's commission. The broker would most likely bargain for a better price for me in order to make a deal. Furthermore, I would save time. Thus, I asked Mr. Goldman to buy the building for me.

The owner was asking for two hundred eighty thousand dollars. Since I was unfamiliar with the real estate market, I called Mr. Miller, because he not only knew the value of real estate property, but how to calculate the cost of a building and figure out what investment the buyer should make in order to make a profit. He came right away and looked at the building. The next day, he called and told me to offer one hundred eighty thousand dollars.

My broker told me that when he offered that price to the owner, the man laughed at him. He told my broker the building had already been sold, and they were waiting for the approval of the mortgage loan at the bank. Hearing this, I said to myself, "Oh no, I have lost a good opportunity."

A contract is a contract only when it is signed, sealed, and delivered, however. A few weeks later, my broker called to tell me the prospective buyer's mortgage had not come through. I told him to get the building for me without delay. He asked how much I was willing to pay. I answered, "I am willing to pay the lowest price you can get it for."

The next day, he came to my office and said he had offered two hundred ten thousand dollars, but the seller wouldn't sell.

I told Mr. Miller what had happened, and he became upset, saying my instruction to my broker had been unprofessional. He added, "You should never have let your broker offer so much. The building is not worth that kind of money."

"Mr. Miller, please listen to me," I said. "I am buying the building not for investment, resale, or rental. I am buying it to have a place to make money with my operation. Paying a little more or less for the building has little to do with the profit or loss of my company. If I pay ten or twenty thousand more than it is worth to a real-estate investor, I can get that money back in one or two months. From that point on, I can continue to make money. Without the larger building, I cannot make as much money because I do not have room to install more production machines."

"Look around more, and you will find a cheaper building," he responded. "Maybe you should move to the suburbs."

I told Mr. Miller one more time, "This building is close to our current plant, and we will not lose employees due to the move. Furthermore, the more I delay, the less money I make. I thank you very much for your concern."

Then I told my broker to buy the building, even if we had to increase our offer by ten thousand dollars or even twenty thousand dollars. In two days he bought the building for me for two hundred thirty thousand dollars. This was just as I expected. I realized that once my broker knew I definitely wanted the building, he would offer the higher price. That way he had a better chance of getting the building and earning more commission.

I had calculated the advantage of moving to a larger building as soon as possible. When I told Mr. Miller that I had paid two hundred thirty thousand dollars, he grew angry with me, saying that I'd overpaid. But his valuation was based on calculations for investors. I repeated that my figures showed that even the higher price was fair, because I could now start to make more money. We closed on the new building in 1974; when we moved to our third building in 1983, we sold it for four hundred thousand dollars.

When we rented our first building, we spent much effort to clean up after the previous tenant, who had been making felt wallpapers. This time, the previous tenant had processed nuts. One might assume the building had to be clean to meet the standards of the food industry. Not so! On the day we took occupancy of the building, Dan, our superintendent, and I drove over and parked our cars in the small parking lot. The first thing we noticed was the marked circle on the garage door, clearly a pitching target.

"Kids have been playing baseball here," I said. Then I saw two broken glass blocks in the window. "They were okay when I first came here," I said. "They must have been cracked recently."

When we walked into the building through the garage door, we found the huge, high open space quite impressive. Then we walked to the back, where Dan almost fell down. The floor of the former nut-processing area was coated with oil and very slippery. Behind the back wall was a large storage room, also used for nuts. We circled the storage area, and Dan noticed one of the electrical boxes on the wall was blocked by something inside the box.

He paused to investigate, as I continued into the older section of the building. Suddenly I heard Dan yell.

"John, you won't believe this! There's a dead mouse in the electric box."

I said to myself, "How could they get away with this?"

The older section had primarily been used for storing equipment, old and new. Now that it had been moved away, we could see the dust between the spaces where the equipment stood was over two inches thick.

The front door was at the corner of the commercial and residential streets. The three adjacent offices ran along the side facing the residential street. Along the commercial street side, the building housed eight small one-room apartments on the second floor. We walked up the stairway at the end of the structure to a hallway. It seemed clean, but the lighting was poor, with two low-wattage bulbs.

When we reached the far end of the hallway, an old lady emerged from her apartment and peered at us for a moment.

"Are you the new owner?" she asked.

"Yes," I said, nodding pleasantly.

"People say you are going to close the apartments. Is that true?"

"Yes. We'll notify everyone."

"Can I please stay here?" she asked.

"I'll talk to you later," I answered.

We walked downstairs, took a look at the office area, then, went back our office to call a professional cleaning service to sanitize the whole building.

Next, I notified the tenants I was evicting them. The apartments were substandard, occupied for the most part by undesirables. Since they knew I meant business, six tenants moved before the end of the month, but two still remained. One was the old woman, and she wanted to stay so badly that she offered to be my eyes and ears in the neighborhood, watching the kids for me.

I hoped we would not have vandalism, but how could I prevent it, with kids all around us in the residential area in the rear? Not only did they play baseball in our parking lot, but when they felt mischievous, they threw rocks at the glass-block windows and floodlights.

For the most part, I felt the kids acted on impulse, not really meaning any harm. Nevertheless, vandalism, like terrorism, is extremely difficult to prevent. Vandals are free to choose the time and place to strike, while potential victims must be prepared to defend themselves day and night.

From the new plant we could hear mothers hollering at their children and saw an old man chasing away the kids whenever he caught sight of them, but what did that accomplish? Nothing. The bicycle tracks over the old man's lawn were made fresh every day.

How could we protect ourselves? I did not think the old woman would be the answer. In theory, I felt, the best way would be to become friends with the neighborhood kids. If they do not hate me, or if I could even get them to like me, they might not think of setting fire to my building or breaking my windows, I reasoned.

Shortly thereafter, I went upstairs to the old woman's apartment and told her, "I am truly sorry, but I have no choice. If you need more time to find a place, I will not rush you." She moved within a few weeks.

When I visited the other apartment, I was surprised to find the apartment clean and nicely furnished. The tenant, a young lady with a baby in her arms, had left the closet open, and I noticed that half of it was full of men's clothing, including a black leather jacket. She told me she could not find a new place to live. Finally, I had to get help from the social worker who handled her case to persuade her to move.

Sunzi wrote: "One who has too much passion toward people will be bothered too much."

While I tackled the apartment problems, we made plans for moving, plotting it out as carefully as if it were a science project. Moving from a small plant to a larger one indicated success, and employees liked to work for a growing company. Everyone was excited and worked hard in preparation for the move.

We planned everything with such precision that we needed only five hours for moving each molding machine, from shutting down in the old plant to starting up in the new one, a truly efficient operation.

We also built a tool room equipped for four or five toolmakers, where they could repair and maintain the molds. A fairly large area in Daniel's office was designated for quality-control instruments and worktables.

We created a new waiting area with chairs, where visitors had to talk to my secretary through a window before they would be allowed entrance; thereby security was much improved. We also bought new furniture for my office, including a sofa and chairs for visitors. We saved our blue sofa bed and put it in the lady's washroom, but we finally let go of the pink dinette set. I knew our operation had made one large step forward.

When we finally settled down in our new building, I often walked to our new tool room to talk to our mold-repair people. One day, I went there at lunch hour. Four men were eating together at one table. The moment I walked in, one smart guy said, "John, I heard you're going to buy a new car."

"Yes. My car is too old now."

Another man asked, "What kind car are you going to buy?"

"I am thinking of a Buick Century," I answered promptly.

They broke into laughter.

"John," one guy said, "that's a small car. We never worked for such a cheap boss. Our old bosses all had big cars." They told the truth, as I knew they all had big cars themselves. Toolmakers made good money, and they liked big cars.

I defended myself. "What do I want a big car for? I don't want to impress anybody, and big cars only waste gas."

"Oh, c'mon," one fellow said. "When we saw you driving that little Montego, we felt ashamed to have a boss who was so tight."

"You guys really think I should buy a big car?" I asked.

They said in one voice, "Oh, yeah."

Every day on my commute, I passed by a Cadillac dealer. That afternoon on my way home, I stopped at the showroom. A short man with gray hair greeted me. He looked like an experienced salesman.

"My name is Sam. Can I help you?"

"I'm just looking," I said casually, and examining the 1975 models.

After a few moments, I guessed he sensed I was serious.

"Come over to my office," he said, "and I'll show you the beautiful features." He started to preach about how luxurious a Cadillac was and why a person should own one.

"Do you have a blue one with the options in stock?" I asked.

Surprised by my question, he said, "If not here, I can get you one very quickly."

I ordered one and would take possession in two weeks. On my way home, I said to myself triumphantly, "That's what they wanted, and that's what they'll get."

Chinese proverb: "From thrift to luxury is easy; from luxury to thrift is hard."

The first thing I did after moving into the building was to hold an open house for the neighbors. They all came: mothers, some fathers, and of course, boys and girls of all ages. We had soft drinks, cookies, candies, and cakes on a Saturday afternoon, when we were not working. Everybody had a chance to see the molding machines. Some kids even took plastic parts as souvenirs. The party went nicely. The neighbors thought at least I was not a bad man, and maybe I was friendly.

Chinese proverb: "Relatives far away are not as important as close neighbors."

At the gathering, I particularly enjoyed meeting a very nice old man who lived in a small apartment behind our plant. He had recently retired. He and I commiserated about the neighborhood children. Coping just with them was easy, he said, but they had friends who came from all over the surrounding area to play. Their parents were not around, so they could do anything and walk away. The worst were the kids who were passersby. They crossed through our parking lot every day and sometimes acted irresponsibly.

In spite of my efforts to be friendly, I learned that a six-year-old boy had rolled up a piece of rag, stuck it under a wooden side door, and lit it. The fire failed to spread, but the residue was obvious. We didn't use that door anyway, so I had workers remove it and brick up the opening. We replaced the broken glass blocks, installed wire covers to protect the floodlights, and repaired the garage door, which had cracked by being used as a pitching target.

The most troublesome problem involved the Saturday night parties. Neighborhood kids hosted their school friends and gathered in our parking lot. Some came on foot, but most came by car and motorcycle. They drank beer and soft drinks and left empty cans all over the lot. The main annoyance came from the loud music that blared half the night. The revelers blasted their car radios with rock music so loud that people on the next block could hear it.

Since we didn't work on weekends and closed the plant at 8 A.M. on Saturday, these parties didn't interfere with us; but we had to clean up the beer cans every Monday morning. We received phone calls from ladies in the neighborhood requesting us to stop the parties. I told them we weren't there on Saturday nights and encouraged them to call the police.

Of course, they were not happy with that answer. One woman came to see me. She said she lived across the street from the parking lot. I could see she was the type who would push as far as she could. She looked like a political worker, neatly dressed, dark hair, with exploring eyes. She told me she was a schoolteacher and came from the East Coast. She demanded that we stop the disturbances.

I told her we would put up No Trespassing and No Loitering signs, and that unlawfully parked cars could be towed away. But the towing company and the police would have to enforce this. Then I said, "If they make noise on Saturday nights, you could call the police. We have to cooperate to stop the disturbances."

"If you don't break up the parties, I will sue you," she said. "Here is my lawyer's phone number. You can have your lawyer call him. If necessary, we'll see you in court."

"If you try to drive us out of the neighborhood, you'll be making a mistake," I told her frankly. "Here we have many jobs for Chicagoans."

Perhaps she thought she might be able to shove me around a little. After this encounter, I never heard from her.

One day, our water chiller, installed near an outside alley, made noise during the night. The older man I had met at our open house called me in the morning to complain. I went over to his apartment and apologized, and we sent people to fix the chiller promptly. At first, he was a little angry, but later he became quite friendly.

During our conversation, I learned his young son, Scott, had been one of the boys playing in our parking lot and was one of the organizers of the ball games and Saturday night get-togethers.

I decided I needed to befriend the boys' ringleader. The next day, a Saturday afternoon, I went to the office to investigate the situation. The kids had already begun to gather. At about four o'clock, three cars had parked in the lot, and five or six fellows stood around their cars.

The baseball-pitching target was still on the garage door, but the lights and windows were in good shape. I nervously thought, "Well, here I am, on the battleground".

Wondering how they would react to me, I strolled over to the boys and said hello. Facing one boy I saw coming from the apartment area, I asked, "Are you Scott?"

He said yes.

"I met your father yesterday. He told me you're a very nice fellow, and a good organizer."

After a friendly conversation about the kids' problem, having no place nearby where they could play ball, I told him, "I don't mind you guys playing ball here. I don't think it's a crime to have a Saturday night party, either, if you put the bottles and cans in the garbage drum we'll provide and keep the music a little lower."

Then, I turned around toward all of them. "This evening you'd better watch out," I said, "I was told that one of the neighborhood women has already called the police, and they are already on the way here. You'd better drive away now and come back later."

They left, and the police arrived shortly thereafter. Finding nothing disturbing, the officers drove away.

From that day, the neighborhood boys regarded me as an ally. Scott turned out to be a congenial and sensible boy who had some influence over the others.

After that weekend, all we had to do was clean up the lot every Monday morning. That was very little to pay for peace of mind and no vandalism.

Sunzi wrote: "Only benevolence and sincerity can manage espionage."

7

Benefits

"Helping people is the root of happiness."

—Chinese proverb

Magenta had been growing slowly but steadily from the very beginning. Three years after we started, we stopped taking on subcontract jobs. A couple of years later, we eliminated most short-run work from the premium people and secured top-notch corporations as our own customers.

To serve them, we now had over forty people working three shifts with ten machines in a plant of twenty-four thousand square feet. Such progress was the result of everyone's effort. Our employees tried hard to do a good job, and thus, helped to build up the company and their own security at the same time.

Of course, all this could never have happened if my investors had not put up their money to help me get my business started.

To show my appreciation for their faith in me and to reinforce their confidence, I began to think of dividends for my investors and added benefits for my employees. I called my accountant and asked if I could begin to issue dividends to my shareholders. After a brief review, my accountant gave me the go-ahead. Thus, we started to issue dividends at the end of 1971, three years from the opening day.

Chinese proverb: "Without going through the penetrating cold, how can we have the plum fragrance wafting to our noses?"

I found myself quite eager to send a check to my schoolmate investor, as he'd been the only one who invested additional money when I desperately needed cash. But to tell the truth, I really didn't feel happy to send money to Mr. Fu. He had refused to help, even though he'd been able. He hadn't cared if I went under, although, at that time, we had supposedly been friends for over twenty years.

The next late spring, I called the annual stockholders' meeting at my house to report what we had done in the past year and what we planned to do next. To my surprise, my rich friend from New York showed up, realizing his investment had not vanished as he originally anticipated. He must have said to himself, "Ah ha! Dividends! I must see what's going on there."

After the meeting, I drove the stockholders to the plant for a tour. They had never seen a manufacturing plant, so I could not expect them to appreciate what I had done with so little money in so short a time. Mr. Fu showed no sign of regret that he had not invested more money. I figured our plant did not impress him, and he did not expect us to become more successful.

Chinese proverb: [It is like] "Playing a harp for a cow."

During the first three years, I had offered some benefits for employees. After my investors had received their due, I began to plan additional benefits for them. Later, I gradually added many more for their security. Mentally, I felt quite comfortable and relaxed. Then, President Nixon visited China, and thus, China opened her doors to the West. I thought of going back for a visit and suggested the idea to June.

She said, "You know I never was crazy about traveling. It's been such a long time for you. You go see your brother and relatives. You'll feel much more at home without me."

"But it will be much more fun if we both go together," I countered.

She replied, "Maybe later. You go first now."

So in 1979, thirty years since I had left home, I joined the first sightseeing tour and left for China. The tour group had about twenty-five people; most were wives and a few men owners of restaurants and stores from Chicago's Chinatown. Except for one man from Shanghai and me from Hobei, all the others were from Guangdong province. The group leader owned a souvenir and bookstore.

On a bright spring day, we flew to Hong Kong and took a train to Guangzhou. At the train station the first people we saw were uniformed police, which made me a little uneasy.

Then we learned that our leader and the Chinese travel agency had gotten their wires crossed, and there was no reservation for us in the hotel. They had to put us up in a meeting hall with twenty-five movable beds lined up like an army barracks under a large picture of Chairman Mao. Ladies slept along the wall and men in one corner. We all had clean white sheets, but for some reason the lights were on all night. So, I covered my head with my raincoat and slept with my day-time clothes on. The next morning most people were already up, when I lifted my raincoat cover, and my companions laughed loudly at my silly way of sleeping.

The leader knew that I was some sort of industrial person and apparently thought I was a big shot. He stood by my bed and said, "You are indeed a good man who can bend and stretch." He was referring to a Chinese proverb, which means that a good man can take on anything, good or bad.

After a few days, we flew to Beijing. We toured the usual famous places, like the emperor's palace, the summer palace, the great wall, North Lake, and restaurants serving famous Beijing foods. I had been to these places before I left China, so I felt sad to notice the deterioration in services.

People's jobs were assigned by their district officials. They could not be fired, and were paid the same amount whether their performance was good or bad. Why should they try to please? Nobody had a smiling face, which made me feel uncomfortable, not welcome or not at home.

From Beijing we took a sleeper train south to Nanking. While our group was touring the well-known spots, I took time to visit my good friends Mr. Liu and his wife An-You. Liu was from my high school, and You was my classmate in college. They still had their house with a beautiful garden, as they were in a large city and not farmland owners.

Here I found my friend Fan, who had loaned me some money for my trip to the U.S. Later, I had been unable to locate him. I wrote him a check right away, for many times more than he gave me, and he was surprised, but, of course, very happy.

The tour continued to some of China's most beautiful places. When the group returned to the U.S. by the way of Hong Kong, I said goodbye to the group members and flew back to Beijing to visit my brother, my sister's son, and her daughter's sons.

I asked to invite them to some famous restaurants, but was told that they had been closed for many years. During the two weeks I stayed, they could only buy spinach and cooking oil for one per person per month, so they could not cook any special treats for their guest, and we had to eat in small restaurants for every meal.

From other relatives I learned that my brother's wife had not been nice to my parents when they were alive; but since my brother lived in a very old apartment and shared a courtyard with three other families, I couldn't help but buy a new condo for him anyway.

But at the end of the journey, I still felt empty, because I could not see the people I loved the most: my father, mother, and sister, all of whom had passed on. I went back too late!

Fortunately, I took loads of pictures to bring back to show June the beautiful sceneries. Now that the door had been opened, I was sure that the country would change rather rapidly, becoming wealthier and modernized. The next time I visited China, I felt sure I would see people eating better foods and wearing colorful clothes instead of drab gray and blue uniforms.

Back at Magenta, our continued growth put me in a festive mood. I wanted to plan a special event to express my gratitude. Just as people observe birthdays to observe the successful completion of another year of life, I decided to host an annual business celebration to acknowledge the successful survival of one more year. How should we do it? I wondered.

I talked about employee Christmas parties with a salesman who came to see me when we moved into our new plant. He told me of a man who gave every employee a turkey at Thanksgiving. He said this man was very tight with his money, but did this every year because it cost him so little and made many people very happy. I liked the idea, so we have given every employee a turkey for Thanksgiving ever since.

Confucius said: "Find the good to follow and use the bad to correct oneself."

But I still needed to decide what kind of party to host. When I was with the Indiana company, I had attended their annual all-employee Christmas party. Several people got drunk before the party was over, and many others were high. They told off-color jokes, and one manager took his secretary to a quiet place to neck. Somehow, the husband of the secretary, who didn't work for the company, came to join the fun and found them together. What an ugly scene!

I noticed that most people had not enjoyed such an undignified event. I promised myself then, I would never host a wild employee party.

After three years in business, we started to give all employees a Christmas bonus a couple of days before Christmas, so they could do some last minute shopping. The day before Christmas, we gave all employees a Christmas lunch during the lunch hour of each shift.

I gave a great deal of thought to the menu for these meals, because of an experience I had had with Art, the president of the aluminum forging company. One year after I left his employ, he invited me to a Christmas lunch at his die shop. When I walked into his plant, I saw people standing at tables covered with white paper, fixing their own sandwiches and drinks. At one end of the tables he had placed five or six bottles of hard liquor; next to the bottles was an ice bucket and a large pitcher of water. I saw no soft drinks.

Along the center of the tables, loaves of sliced rye bread were piled high near a chunk of butter formed like a tree stump. A few knives were scattered around the butter, but no forks or spoons. Next to large salt-and-pepper shakers sat a huge ball of raw ground sirloin with slices of raw onion behind it. A plate of various cheeses cut into cubes and slices gave off a strong odor that mixed with the smell of coffee, which was brewing to the side.

I found Art and said Merry Christmas.

He greeted me with his charming smile. "John! I'm glad you came. Let me show you how to eat this good stuff."

He picked up a slice of rye bread and put it on his left palm, which reminded me that the tip of his left middle finger had been cut off by a punch press years before. He grabbed a big handful of raw ground sirloin, rolled it into a patty with his right hand, and slapped it onto the center of the bread. He spread the meat over the bread fairly evenly with his right thumb and sprinkled some salt, and a lot of pepper over the meat. Then he moved two steps over, picked up two slices of raw onion, and smacked them on the meat. He turned, grinned at me, and said, "Look. You eat it like this." He opened his large mouth and took a big bite from one corner of the open-faced sandwich.

I smiled at him and said, "Wow!" I waited for him to move away, then made a Swiss cheese on rye sandwich and poured a cup of coffee. I rarely ate cheese and only occasionally drank coffee, but I couldn't eat anything else on the tables.

Art believed everyone should eat the way German tool makers do and enjoy it. This luncheon left a deep impression on me. I decided Magenta's Christmas lunch should include food to please everyone. Thus we served fried chicken, roasted beef au jus, potato salad, pickles, and Kaiser rolls. Since we had many Polish workers, we added Polish sausage and sauerkraut. I ate with the first-shift people at noon. I knew I had done a good job, when I saw some young men helping themselves to second helpings.

This meal was worth my best effort, I realized, because it made me happy that my employees were happy.

Determining the amount of the Christmas cash bonus for each employee was no simple matter. We had to keep in mind two things. First was the basic principle of giving out benefits to employees. Once the system was set up, it should be continued and not be taken away from the employees; otherwise, morale would be damaged.

The other was the fairness of distribution. The only tangible factors we could use to determine the amount for each employee were length of service and attendance records, but we still liked to take into consideration intangible factors like performance and contribution. Of course, the job level was a basic factor. Foremen received the biggest bonuses, and the newly hired got a minimum bonus.

Management should never expect employees not to know how much their coworkers earn. I believed that, sooner or later, everyone would know everyone else's bonus, and all my decisions regarding employee pay were based on the assumption that everyone knew who made what. I could tell we had calculated bonus amounts fairly, because after the first two years we heard no complaints about who got more or less.

The Christmas bonus was unexpected income for our new employees, who were not told about it, when they came to work. We also promoted most of our employees of various levels. Even our long-standing employees were not always sure from year to year how much they would receive. Everyone was grateful for the extra cash, and I hoped the holiday bonus would be one more reason for employees to stay with us long-term.

I hosted a second annual Christmas party as well, this one for management and outside people who had worked with us during the year, our bankers, accountant, attorneys, advertising agent, consulting engineers, and so on.

At the end of the first year in business, we held this party in a restaurant. We invited only about ten people and sat at one large table. We had fine food and good conversation, but after the dinner, somehow June and I didn't feel as if we had had fun.

After that, we held our parties in our home. For the first few years, since we didn't have many people, we didn't feel crowded, although our house was modest. We had good times, played charades, and even danced a little.

"How is business?" a friend of June's who sold real estate, asked her over lunch.

"Very good," June answered.

"You should move to a larger house," Annabeth said.

"Why? We're comfortable where we are," she responded. "Of course, unless you can find us a house on the lake."

"I might just do that," she claimed.

Six months later, Annabeth called my wife. "I found your house on the lake."

My wife was surprised, but Annabeth insisted she take a look. "You don't have to buy it. I'll pick you up at one o'clock."

At one-thirty, I received a call from June. "I am at a nice house on the lake," she said. "It's just perfect for us, and you must come and see it. Of course, we don't have to buy it."

I was busy at the plant and couldn't get away till three o'clock. The moment I walked through the front door, I saw the beautiful blue water through the large picture window in the living room. I was sold then and there. Annabeth showed me the backyard with ninety-four feet of lake frontage, and how the corner of the sunroom stood only about thirty feet from the water.

"How much?" I asked.

She told me the price.

"What should we offer?"

She laughed. "You don't make an offer. You buy or don't. If you wait till tomorrow, after I've listed this house on the market, you'll have to bid against many other people who've been waiting for houses on the lake."

We went to the kitchen, where I picked up the phone and called Bernie, my accountant. He said he thought I could afford it.

Then, I dialed my banker. "You think I can get a mortgage?"

"If it's all right with you and Bernie, it's all right with me," he said. "I know that area."

Annabeth could not reach the owner in Florida until six o'clock. Even so, she said that was the fastest sale she'd ever made.

From the year 1977 on, our Christmas parties have been in our house on Lake Michigan. During the parties, everyone mixed their own cocktails and their wife's drinks. They could sit anywhere in the house comfortably, and talked in large and small groups.

We always had a buffet dinner that included a variety of foods, so guests could pick anything they liked and fill their plates as often as they wished. We selected roasted beef tenderloin as the main dish, as most Americans like beef best. Five Chinese dishes, each picked as the specialty from one restaurant, were lined up as accompaniments. Often, I had to pick up foods from two or three places on the afternoon before the party. We added a casserole, a green salad, and a fruit salad.

The fruit salad was our house specialty, and many guests asked for the recipe. We had to tell them we did not have a formal recipe, but just mixed the fruits by our intuition. We used fresh green and red grapes cut in halves, tangerines, black cherries, canned litchi nuts, diced dates, marshmallows, and sour cream. Marshmallow made it sweet, and sour cream made it mellow; but we made sure we added a little litchi-nut juice to dilute the sour cream. Otherwise, the salad would be too rich. We had to be careful not to get tangerine or cherry juice in the salad, when we had to use canned tangerines or cherries. We made the salad in the morning, and kept it in the refrigerator till the party time. That way the dates would evenly distribute their flavor.

After sweets and coffee or tea, we gathered for entertainment. We tried many different things for entertaining, but found the most successful were magicians and a gift-grabbing game. To play the game, people sat in a large circle, and gift packages were piled up like a hill in the center. People took turns throwing a pair of giant-sized dice. One who got seven, eleven, or doubles won the right to grab one package from the pile, or snatch one from any person who had won gifts.

This game turned adults into children. Our banker, Byron, greedily searching for the largest bag, sent us into paroxysms of laughter when he tore open the wrapping paper to reveal five pounds of peanuts in shells.

I have always been grateful that we bought the house, because June loved and enjoyed it so much. A few years thereafter, she got cancer and passed away. I regret deeply she did not like to travel, but I respected her reason: She thought the most comfortable place was her own home. Luckily she enjoyed nice clothes from stores like Neiman-Marcus, and so was somewhat rewarded for her labor and contributions to our company, giving the husband she left behind some peace of mind.

One can never imagine how sad it is to lose one's wife. The feeling of knowing that she would never come back was indescribably painful. When I sat at our patio watching the moonrise, I murmured to myself, "She'll never see this moonlight over the gentle waves on the lake again."

Chinese proverb: "There are three saddest things: Lost mother when young; lost wife at middle age; and lost son when old."

I heard about the death of a plant superintendent of a large plastic-molding company, someone for whom our foreman used to work. The superintendent had labored long hours every day, six days a week. Often he added Sundays when needed. This superintendent drank beer every day after work to relieve his tension. According to Daniel, by the time the superintendent retired at sixty-five, he looked like an old man.

When he passed away a few years later, he had not saved much money and left practically nothing to his family. His bosses had the reputation of being greedy, and while they became wealthy and took good care of themselves, they did not offer a pension or a profit-sharing plan to their workers. I felt this was totally indecent and unfair.

I determined this would never happen to my foremen or other employees. First, I decided to stick to a five-day workweek. Only for urgent requirements would we work on Saturdays, and never on Sunday.

We set our wages higher than those of other plastic-molding companies in our area, including the one with a union.

"Your pay will be the equivalent of, or close to the pay for six days in other shops in this area," I told my foremen. I told my workers, "I want you to work around the house or go shopping with your wife on Saturdays. Go to the zoo with your kids on Sundays, and come to work on Monday fresh and rested. If I find out you were moonlighting on weekends, you will be fired."

To produce six days' worth of goods in five days, we had to install one extra machine for every five machines. The capital investment turned out to be quite large, and we used up a great deal of valuable space. But we did it, because I was committed to my employees' quality of life.

Besides establishing a healthy working schedule as company policy, I offered health insurance to every employee a few months after we completed the first year. Originally, since the cost was low, I thought the company would pay all the premiums, but after more careful thinking, I decided to have employees pay two dollars per week. I initiated this copayment policy to remind them that they had health insurance, that the insurance cost money, and that the company paid for most of it.

Another reason was that some employees' husbands worked at other companies, and they were already covered by their husbands' insurance policy. We didn't want them to have double insurance. Although two dollars was a small amount, nobody wanted to waste money; thus they would not enroll in our policy. Furthermore, the premium would certainly be increased at some point in the future. Once the cost became too high, the company would have to increase the share of the employees' payment.

Mencius, Confucius's most influential follower, said: "[True] Men all have the heart that cannot stand the suffering of other men."

The sad demise of the hardworking superintendent haunted me. After about three years in business, when I felt confident our company would survive, I began thinking about the future of our employees. I believed that everyone should be able to leave something behind after laboring a whole lifetime. A retirement plan would benefit not only employees but also the company. It would give employees confidence in the company, promote loyalty, and encourage them to stay for life.

I compared the advantages of profit sharing and pension plans. Most large corporations had pension plans. The corporation had to put up a certain amount of money each year for the plan, whether it had made a profit or not. The employees were assured of having a certain percentage of regular income after retirement, but received very little if they didn't live long. On the other hand, the employee could expect to receive income for as long as he or she lived. Supplemented by Social Security, the pension plan did provide employees security after retirement.

But such defined benefit payments could put a small company in big trouble, if the company became unprofitable. In the event a small company lost money for a few years, these benefit payments could actually put the company out of business. Furthermore, some employees preferred to receive bigger lump-sum payments at retirement, which they could then use to start a small business of their own. Many people wished to do something on their own, but didn't dare sacrifice their bread-and-butter job before retirement.

With a profit-sharing plan, the company would contribute a certain amount of money to the fund each year, the amount depending on that year's earnings. If the company made no money, it didn't have to put out anything. This made the company more secure. Since our company had been profitable, and I expected the trend to continue for years, I believed our profit-sharing plan would accumulate money for the employees.

Seeing their savings grow in the profit-sharing fund year after year, the employees would feel they truly belonged to the organization, and gain confidence in their own future. As a result, employees would become more loyal and the morale would be high, particularly when, at any time of the year, they could see how much money was saved under their name.

Under a pension plan, employees could not see anything in their name, and no one could be sure how long he or she would live.

Confucius said: "A gentleman accomplishes what he is going to say and then says it."

We decided on the profit-sharing plan in 1972. Under our plan so far, Magenta has put about ten percent of annual pre-tax earnings into the profit-sharing fund. The more money an employee made, the greater his or her share.

To invest the fund was not a simple matter. Being public money, the employees' fund had to be treated prudently. Our stockholder Mr. Fu, my wealthy friend in New York, had been successful investing in growth common stocks. I invited him to be a trustee with me for the fund.

"We must not take risks with our employees' fund, but at the same time, I want to make money for them," I told him.

"I am a firm believer in investing in long-term growth common stocks," Mr. Fu replied. "If we diversified into more growth stocks, you would not need to invest in bonds or CDs."

With Mr. Fu's successful track record, I felt confident that if I invested all the money in large, established, growing corporations, the fund would be safe and expand, and our employees would have a comfortable retirement. This has proven to be the case over the years, and makes me feel extremely happy and satisfied.

Of course, any plan has disadvantages and advantages. The disadvantage of our profit-sharing plan was that because of the attractiveness of the growing savings in the fund, we found it difficult to get rid of undesirable employees, particularly the mediocre workers. The law does not allow the firing of employees with inferior performance without legal cause. I didn't know what to do when they stayed on and on to see their savings grow, in spite of their not deserving it.

One incident is worth mentioning. A couple of years after we started our profit-sharing plan, a reliable and steady female worker all of a sudden quit and would not tell me why. Since she insisted on not saying a word, I suspected she had found a better-paying job and didn't want to say so. Anyway, nobody ever heard from her after that.

Several months after she left, a coworker told my secretary that this woman had quit because she needed the savings in her profit-sharing fund to pay for a dental operation. It would be a shame if that story were true. I could have helped her borrow money from the bank we used. If the rumor was true, then we lost a good worker because of the profit-sharing plan.

Regardless, after setting up the profit-sharing plan, I felt more comfortable about the employees' future, and I was sure none would be like the hardworking superintendent who died with nothing.

A few years after we moved to our second plant, I noticed that quite a few employees, particularly women, had become overweight during the years with us. Good health is important to everybody, and healthy employees meant a steady workforce for the company. Overweight is the first cause of poor health, and I thought I should help them to reduce.

My first idea was to start a weight-loss incentive program. I thought such a program would encourage those who wanted to lose weight, as they could be inspired by others to reduce together and, in the meantime, receive some rewards. Anyone who wished to lose weight could sign up and weigh in. The company would give a ten-dollar reward for every pound a participant reduced in one month. I talked to our office manager, Geri, and she liked the idea. I asked her to put out a bulletin explaining the program and asking people to sign up.

A month passed, but not one person signed up for the program. Much puzzled, I told Geri to ask around in the factory to find out why nobody wanted to participate. I thought they might not have noticed the bulletin, but I was wrong. After talking to a couple of overweight ladies, she found out they thought it was a good program, but would never let the boss know just how much they weighed!

I asked Geri to persuade some employees to participate, but still no one wanted their coworkers to know their weight. It didn't occur to me at the time to arrange for Geri or another trusted woman to be the only one to record the weights. Thus a good thought became a total failure!

This matter of health reminded me of my own experience. When we opened the doors for business, I had to do almost everything myself, because we were operating on a shoestring. Naturally, I worked long hours every day, including weekends. In addition, I had many worries and tensions. In two years, I'd become literally worn out. I caught a cold and, then, the Hong Kong flu. I was so sick I could not sit in the chair in my office. I lay on the old faithful sofa, and put the telephone on the floor by my head, as I didn't have a coffee table.

A compassionate doctor came to my office and gave me some shots. It was the last house call by a doctor I know of. Still, I remained physically weakened.

Friends said that since I worked too hard, naturally I got tired. "Just relax and take it easy a little," they advised. I found their counsel vague and impractical. What did they mean, "Take it easy a little"? What was I supposed to do?

I began to examine my lifestyle and habits. When I was in college, the dean of physical education taught us many ways for healthy living. The most important one was to exercise every day. I never had a problem with that, because I always liked participating in sports. I was expert in none, but tried a little of them all.

After college, I played tennis occasionally, but ever since starting my own business, I had had no exercise at all. I thought I had no time for it, and the neglect had caught up with me. So I told myself, "The first thing I must do is to exercise every day."

What exercise? I had no spare time, and therefore, could not play golf or even tennis. I never liked swimming; the water always seemed too cold. Even long walks took hours. Exercise machines seemed unnatural to me. Thus, it became obvious that the only effective and efficient exercise I could take was jogging. I knew I could do it, because my doctor had pronounced my heart in good shape during my annual physical.

I did not like the idea of people watching me jog, so I started in my backyard. In the beginning, I jogged for only five minutes, but in two months reached thirty minutes for about two miles. I was slow but kept my pulse up.

Since then, I have been able to jog every day. Before I knew it, I didn't feel so tired anymore. When I got angry with somebody, or when I had a problem, thirty minutes of jogging put everything back into perspective.

Magazine articles say that doctors believe exercise three times a week is good enough for the heart. That might be true, but in order to keep my stamina up, body limber, and thinking alert and sharp, I must exercise every day except when I'm sick. To prevent knee or ankle injuries, I minimize my bouncing during jogging.

Since jogging has done miracles for me, I plan to jog throughout my life. I figure if I jogged yesterday and today, I should be able to jog tomorrow. I will count one day at a time.

In the meantime, I often recommended exercise in any form to employees as well as friends. The headquarters of large corporations often have exercise rooms equipped with machines, but our employees are mostly factory workers who labor physically every day. They'd rather go home and have a glass of beer. We have only a few office employees, so to have an exercise room on the premises is not justified. Besides, for them to jog or walk in their neighborhood costs nothing. The company is happy to pay managers' health club fees, if they go there to exercise regularly. We don't pay for golf-club fees though.

Most people ignore my advice, however. Only one manager who had not exercised for years listened to my advice and started to jog three times a week. Our president, who used to train on exercise equipment every other day, has been exercising daily because of my encouragement. So far no one else has listened, and the overweight people grow more obese. We'll have to keep working on this project.

> **Chinese proverb: "Walk a hundred steps after each meal, and you will live to ninety-nine years old."**

8

Human Behavior

"Rivers and mountains can evolve, but human character is difficult to change."

—Chinese proverb

In the 1960s and early 1970s, American companies did not have much global competition, and some companies were still managed in the old-fashioned way: If the custom molders wanted to establish a good business relationship with the large corporations that used plastic molded parts or components, they normally had to entertain the corporations' buyers.

I heard of a large plastic molding company that did considerable work for a television manufacturer. The owner of the molding company shipped large appliances to the home of the buyer of the electronics company. Another molding shop, the owner of which I knew personally, gave a huge television to the buyer for a radio manufacturer.

At Magenta, we never did anything like that. We were in our early years and not in a position to make big deals with large molded plastics users such as television or radio manufacturers.

By the time, we bought out Mr. Abrams, the molding broker, we began to take people out for lunch or dinner. The buyer for one vending machine manufacturer was a very nice man, understanding, and kind. June and I took him and his wife to a German restaurant quite a few times. We also did a little work for a radio manufacturer. The buyer was a friendly older man, and I liked him as a person. Whenever he went away for vacation, he always brought back a small souvenir for me. June and I invited him and his wife out for dinner several times before he retired. Even after his retirement, I continued to send him a fruitcake for Christmas.

One man at this radio company was not so nice. We were molding a component of a radio for them. This fellow, a quality-control inspector, telephoned me directly from their out-of-town plant. He told me they had received parts out of specification and asked me to go to his plant and see those parts.

I drove ninety minutes to see him, and learned the parts deviated on one dimension from the engineering drawing from which the mold was made, and that dimension should not have been there in the first place. In the very beginning, we'd asked them to eliminate that dimension, because it had no affect on the function of the part. But they had done nothing about it, because the engineer did not want to stick his neck out for the drawing change. The inspector was well aware of the situation; they had used many parts like that before without any problem. I took the man to lunch, and after he drank a martini and ate a big steak, he suddenly stopped worrying about the so-called defect. It was truly disgusting!

After about two months, he called me again with the same complaint. I told him frankly, "Joe, the problem is the same as last time. You do not need me to come to your plant. That would waste most of the day for me. Can you do me a favor? Pass the shipment, and I will make dinner reservations at the same steak restaurant for you and your wife."

He accepted my offer; what a pity it was!

By the time, we were firmly established in the 1980s, many modern industries and well-managed companies had begun to use molded plastic components, and lavish entertainment went out of fashion. We liked to treat customers to lunch and dinner, as was the standard and accepted practice among all companies. I thought this was a good idea, because it gave both the user and the supplier the opportunity to talk about business as well as become acquainted personally. Gifts of any kind were not permitted.

To show my appreciation for the help and cooperation of our customers' engineers and buyers, I had been sending them Christmas fruitcakes for a good many years. The cakes proved much more practical and ecologically sound than Christmas cards, which were more expensive and time consuming to select, sign, seal, and mail, and would only be thrown away, wasting paper. When we ordered fruitcakes, the supplier did everything, including shipping.

The gesture cost little and could never influence a buyer to give me a molding job. A Christmas fruitcake was like the Thanksgiving turkey I gave my employees; it would not stop them from quitting, if they wanted to.

But the management of the large corporations did not see it that way. They allowed Christmas cards because they were of no value after the holidays, yet they did not permit even a small gift like fruitcake.

One time, the Kentucky plant sent a new engineer to see us and discuss a new project that had been assigned to him. He was clearly a young farmer-turned-engineer. I took him to a Chinese restaurant for lunch. He said he'd never been to one before. I suggested a shrimp dish, but he did not want it, saying, "I have never eaten shrimp. I'd rather stick to meat and potatoes." He was a polite man, and everything was strictly for business.

During the Christmas holidays, I still sent fruitcakes to all the engineers and buyers of our customers. Although any gift was against the rules, nobody paid much attention to fruitcakes, and everybody was happy.

I sent a fruitcake to this new engineer, too. He turned the cake over to his boss and used me to let his employer know what an honest man he was. Oh, did I get a long letter from his boss!

Chinese proverb: "Even the Emperor's officials do not beat a man who is offering a present."

This philosophy did not hold true with this young man. This proverb wobbled in another case with regard to a book. I always preached to our employees to maintain a positive mental attitude, as I have found for myself that optimism strengthens perseverance. Thus, I had given out to my friends over a dozen copies of an inspirational book emphasizing a positive mental attitude.

I received a phone call from one friend who said, "John, thank you for the book. But do you think I need that?" Before I could explain, he continued, "Oh, I'm just kidding. Thank you very much."

I knew this man well and believed he did worry about whether I thought he really needed to improve his attitude. The fruitcake and the book taught me to be careful in giving gifts.

Confucius said: "Every conduct should be in moderation, not to extremes.

Corporate customers forbade me to send fruitcakes to their engineers and buyers, and after that incident, I followed their advice. But I still feel that the business life would be much more fun if I could give my associates some nibbles at Christmas time. Everybody would be happier.

Corporate rules permitted meals, so I usually invited out-of-state customers' buyers and engineers to nice restaurants. Sometimes we took the people from our Kentucky customer to a play after dinner, not because their corporation was our best customer, but because these people were so decent and sincere.

One engineer particularly liked Chinese food. Since he was such a good eater, I, too, ate more when I lunched with him. He never helped us get any business, but we became good dining companions. I often took him to a small Chinese restaurant named Peter Lo's, my favorite place. We would go to a grocery store across the street from the restaurant to buy a six-pack of cold beer, then walk to the restaurant after the lunch crowd had left.

We would order several servings of steamed dumplings in addition to three or four dishes. Steamed, boiled, or fried dumplings are the most favored food among northern Chinese, and my dining companion acquired the taste from me. As we enjoyed dishes with shrimp, beef, pork, and chicken, all mixed with vegetables, we talked, ate, and drank till late afternoon. By that time, we'd nearly finished all the food, and he would have drunk five cans of beer, and I one.

We also treated our suppliers, service people, and personal friends to lunch. During the meal we might discuss business, current affairs, new technology, or just trade gossip. I always paid the bill, as I figured if someone was willing to visit me or talk about things concerning our operations, at least I should pay for lunch.

Usually my guest said, "John, let me pay this time."

"It's not the money," I always responded. "It's just to show my appreciation that you spent time and took the effort to come. Besides, you would have to make an expense report, and I don't have to."

To social friends, I would say, "For you, this is money after tax. For me, this is money before tax, one dollar worth more than a dollar." I hoped my friends would appreciate this. It was not my intention to throw money around or show off; I believed treating people to a meal now and then was the least expensive way to build friendships. Who knew whether someone might do me a favor or offer me a helping hand someday? If a business opportunity arose, they might tell me first.

I also extended this policy to consultants. For example, a friend recommended a small specialty machine shop to us. The owner designed and built equipment, machines, and fixtures for automation on production operations. When we had a project or a production problem, we usually called him in to see if he could make something for us. He was always very cooperative, and we became friends.

Once, we had a project, and he came in three or four times to discuss it with us, but we couldn't decide on any equipment, so he went off with nothing. When he left my office the last time, I thanked him for his effort. After he was out of our plant, I instructed my secretary to send him a check for four hundred dollars, a fair amount for the time he had spent. When he received the check, he called to say he was surprised and appreciative.

Another time, I invited an engineer to come in to consult on a project. He gave me his idea, which I did not like, although he impressed me with his knowledge. I forgot to ask about his fee, but sent two hundred dollars to his office. That made him looked good, although the money didn't go in his pocket.

A couple of years later, I met him at a party. He made a point of walking over to me, and we had a nice conversation.

Another engineer made a sketch for me. I didn't like his idea and asked him how much I owed. He said two hundred dollars. I sent him three hundred dollars, because I knew he'd spent much more time than he'd charged me for. All these things cost us very little but created good feelings among everyone concerned.

Confucius said: "Being generous you will be able to use people effectively."

Of course, not everyone shares this philosophy. Many Scrooges exist in the real world. One miserly man I had known for years owned a successful industrial-supply company. I had bought supplies from him that amounted to quite a large sum. When he came by trying to sell me something, I often took him to lunch. He liked to talk, and I always learned a lot from him about industry innovations and news on companies and people we both knew. Naturally, we became business friends.

One day, during a conversation in my office, he invited me to see his newly built home in a prestigious northern suburb. He said to me, "John, I can invite you to see my house only because I trust you. I would never invite anybody else to see it, because I'm afraid they would be jealous and think I make too much money."

Although I was busy, I accepted his invitation out of curiosity. When I arrived I saw not a house, but a mansion. It was situated on a five-acre green lawn fenced off with large shade trees all around the back border. The property featured a monumental front gate, flanked by two high towers. He told me the towers were for his daughter and son, each of whom occupied one as their private quarters.

Passing through the entrance hallway, we reached a spacious living room. The new furniture looked luxurious. He introduced me to his wife, who was sitting on the sofa. The back wall of the living room was made of glass. We walked out of the living room through a glass door to a spacious patio with a roomy sitting area near a large swimming pool. The colorful, fluffy lawn chairs looked brand new as well.

"What a beautiful place," I remarked.

"Thank you," he said. Then he paused. "Hey, if you ever want to swim, you are welcome to come here any Sunday after lunch."

His invitation sent a chill down my spine. After all the nice lunches I had treated him to throughout the years, he would not even ask me to have a hot dog with them before swimming! They hadn't even offered me a cold drink, although it was a warm day.

Everybody needs money to live, but I could never imagine any man could be so greedy. If anyone had told him he could not take his money with him when he's gone, he would be the type to say, "Really? Then, I am not going."

This reminded me that a few years before, he and his wife had gone to Florida for a conference, and she lost their camera. "I almost killed her," he had told me.

Another incident I found chilling involves a buyer and engineer who traveled to Chicago from Ohio. For some reason they had transferred two molding jobs to their East Coast plant, and the men responsible for procuring these components had come to Chicago to discuss some problems.

I treated them to a French dinner, as they had requested. Then, I drove them back to their five-star hotel.

On the way, the buyer asked, "John, where's the library?"

I thought he was joking. "What do you mean?"

"You know, something good-looking," he answered vaguely.

When I realized what they had in mind, it startled me. I had heard that some buyers would come to a new city, away from home, and ask for girls, but I had never met people like that before. Being that this was the first time these men had met me, I felt they surely had guts to request such a thing. I told them I had no idea and added, "I hear this hotel is a lively place at night. You can try your luck here." Then, I left.

The next year, I lost those two jobs.

Confucius said: "The *Book of Odes* has three hundred poems which can be summed up in one sentence: 'Think no evil.'"

Money makes some people do strange things. A few years after we started our business, June and I went to a pancake house for Sunday brunch. We met a friend of mine with his wife and two young boys. We sat next to their booth and talked a little about their children's school.

After a few minutes, he asked me, "John, do you charge your family dining out to your expense account?"

I answered without thinking, "No. Why?"

"Why not?" he countered.

This friend, the president and shareholder of a large packaging company, told me he always charged all his family's restaurant tabs to his company expense account as entertaining costs. Apparently, he didn't think it was a big deal.

If I'd said that his policy was neither honest nor fair to other shareholders, I would have insulted him. Had I told him the idea had never occurred to me, he would have thought me naive.

When we came home, I calculated his probable dining expenses, just to satisfy my curiosity. I assumed his family went out for dinner three times a week, twice to inexpensive family-style restaurants and once to some stylish place. For a family of four at early 1980s prices, the cost would most likely run about one hundred sixty dollars a week, or about eight thousand dollars a year.

I guessed in his tax bracket he would have to earn close to eleven thousand dollars to pay for the dining out. With his salary, bonus, dividends, and returns on other investments, eleven thousand dollars was probably a very small part of his total income, considering the principles he sacrificed.

To be honest is good. It creates self-respect and self-confidence. One can look one's children straight in the eyes with a clear conscience. Such freedom is worth more than eleven thousand dollars.

Furthermore, this man's secretary or bookkeeper would know he charged his family's dining expenses to the company. She wouldn't say anything while she worked for him, but one day, if she became angry with the company or with him, she could inform the IRS. Why give one's shortcomings to somebody else to hold on to?

A partner in another plastic molding company was a good friend of mine, and we always helped each other whenever possible. Once, I sat in his office discussing a foreman we both knew. Somehow we got on the subject of heavy taxes, and I learned something even more serious.

"This is a weird game," he said. "On the books, we are making money. But where is it? I can't draw money from the company."

"I feel the same way," I said.

He leaned over and spoke in a confidential tone. "John, I have a friend who is a hardware dealer. He can send your company a ten-thousand-dollar invoice on hardware items. After your company pays him the ten thousand dollars, he will give eight thousand dollars cash back to you. This is one way to take some money out of the company and not have to pay tax. This man is reliable."

In the early 1980s, eight thousand dollars was a good amount of money. After a few seconds, I said, "My friend, that involves too much risk and too little gain. I do not need money that badly right now."

My friend seemed surprised and disappointed. "It's up to you. I'm only trying to help."

Chinese proverb: "You can cover up the fire, but cannot hide the smoke."

All this improper conduct is a response to high taxation, but people react differently. I would never have imagined such a scheme as a way to avoid taxes. My New York friend, Mr. Fu, once said to me, "I like to pay taxes. The more the better, because that means I made more and will have more left."

Of course, at that time, the income tax rate was low, and he paid capital gains taxes at an even lower rate. In the 1990s, the government raised taxes for businesses and high-income people. My accountant told me a client of his got so mad about the tax increases that he went to Florida to play golf for two weeks. "Heck, why should I work so hard just to pay taxes to support those who don't work?" he remarked.

This idea of making less to pay less tax is not sound unless a person really hates to work. Even if he has to pay taxes at a higher rate, to work and expand his business is still justified. As long as he can do it, he most likely keeps more than if he had made less income and paid less taxes.

Once, our banker, our accountant, and I had a luncheon conference. Bernie brought up the unfairness of the tax hike for the rich. After he and Byron joked around a little, I said, "Do you know the best way to solve the high tax problem?"

They looked at me and said no, waiting for a serious answer.

"The only way to beat it is to make more profit."

They all laughed.

Months later, when I met with Byron again, he told me he used my remark on how to beat high taxes in a speech he'd presented at a meeting. He hadn't considered it a joke after all.

For my personal income tax, my accountant did save me some money years ago, in the 1980s, when he suggested I buy some tax shelters. Later on, the government disallowed tax shelters.

Some people purposely mortgage their house to use the interest they pay on the mortgage as a tax deduction. Evidently, they don't realize that the interest they must pay is higher than the tax savings they receive from the interest.

Many people make donations to their favorite charities. That is a good thing, because the donations benefit the recipients and thus society, and also made the donors happy. Sometimes, however, people make tax-deductible donations just to save taxes. They overlook the fact that they have to donate a lot more money than they can save from the donation. Perhaps someone who is famous and important can donate his or her collectible belongings to a museum or institution at fabulous values and save taxes accordingly. But I am not a celebrity. I put a very small value on the old clothes we donate to the Salvation Army.

Investing in growth common stocks, preferably those that issue no dividends, seems to be the only way left to save on income tax, as capital-gains taxes have always been lower than the rate for ordinary income. Such tax savings apply to income earned from personal investments, but don't help to reduce taxes on the income made on salary or from a manufacturing business.

We elected to organize our company under subchapter S, which helped to eliminate the double taxing on corporate income. A company under subchapter S must follow many rules and operate under certain restrictions. I always believed a person should use his or her time and intelligence finding ways to make more money in business, and should not waste time and brain power trying to save money by searching for loopholes to avoid taxes, or by finding ways to take advantage of others, or by hunting for bargains.

Following this principle, I reached my conclusion on taxes: Pay the taxes according to the rules. This policy gives the owner and company management peace of mind. Only a mind free of guilt and scheming can concentrate on pursuing growth and prosperity.

> **Confucius said: "Looking for petty gains, your important tasks will not be successful."**
> **Chinese proverb: "Petty gains are never worth the effort."**

During my second year in business, an Internal Revenue Service agent walked into my office and wanted to check my tax return. The agent, a young woman fresh out of college, was friendly and easygoing. I fully cooperated with her work. After she looked over my return, she asked for my gasoline pump receipts. I could not remember why I'd saved all those receipts, but I did have them. She looked at them one by one until she was satisfied that I'd charged gasoline for only one car. I presumed some people filled up their family car and charged it to their company expense accounts.

She seemed quite pleasant, and I invited her to a simple lunch. Upon returning from lunch, she told me that one section of my tax calculation had been incorrect. I asked my accountant to adjust my return according to her instructions. Then we found out the government had to send us a thirty-eight-dollar refund.

When I walked out of 'The Talker's plant and started my own business, I didn't tell anyone, including coworkers, customers, suppliers, or mutual friends, where I was going. Of course, I made an exception for my coworker investor.

The Talker needed nearly two years to find out where I had gone, although my plant was only two miles from his office. One day, he came to my office with a young man and asked if I'd seen his closure specification book. I presumed he was implying that I had stolen his book. I told him I had not taken even one piece of paper from his company.

He left my office apparently baffled, but the next day called and said he had found his book.

When we moved to our second plant, he suddenly appeared in my office without calling first. I offered him a seat on my blue sofa bed. He said quietly, "I'm on the street. I left my company."

"I am sorry to hear that," I said without expression.

After being silent for a few moments, he asked, "Is there anything I can do for you?"

This man surely had guts, asking for a job from me!

He then continued with some degree of confidence. "I know the people at an Indiana company, and I can get jobs for you."

"Fine," I said. "Why don't you be our representative to get some work from this company? I will pay you the usual five percent commission."

"Good! Thank you very much," he said, and left quickly.

People said I was too forgiving. Before long, The Talker obtained a molding job for us from that Indiana company. After a couple of years, the customer took the job to their own molding plant. The Talker hasn't done anything for us since.

When we moved to our third plant, The Talker unexpectedly stopped by to say hello. We conversed for a few minutes in my office. Before he left, he said, "John, you certainly did a good job."

I thanked him.

Chinese proverb: "Ten years you lived at the east side of the river, next ten years you lived on the west side of the river."

The saying refers to the Yellow River, but it means that no matter what we do or say, ten years hence everything might be changed.

On some occasions, during the early years of my life, various people belittled me. I tried hard to convince myself that my feelings had not been hurt. These incidents must have bothered me at least a little bit, though; otherwise, why should I still remember them? Nevertheless, I never harbored bad feelings toward people who made silly remarks.

For instance, Jerry Logan, the man in charge of the Impact Extrusion Department at the Indiana company, totally ignored my suggestion and quipped, "If you are so smart, why aren't you a millionaire?"

I have fantasized about inviting him to come and see my plant, but such a gesture would have been childish. After I left Indiana and worked in Chicago, I maintained friendly relations with Mr. Stewart, the president of the Indiana company. When the Indiana company went out of business, he took a position with a small aluminum-fabricating company in Chicago. One hot summer day, June and I visited a friend of hers near his neighborhood. We stopped by to see his new house.

We sat on the porch, Mr. Stewart on a lounge chair, June and I on two rattan chairs, and Mrs. Stewart standing by a counter. She served a drink to her husband, then turned and said to us, "Don't you want some lemonade?"

Since she said, "Don't you want," we didn't feel comfortable saying yes, so we said, "No, thank you." But we were really hot and thirsty.

"What are you doing now?" he asked.

"I'm with a plastic molding company," I replied.

June injected, "He always wanted to have his own business."

The boss's wife thought the idea was so absurd, she sneered and made a derisive sound. All she knew about me was that I had worked for her husband at the Indiana company as an engineer. How could she be so sure that it was utterly ridiculous for me to think about having my own business?

At the Indiana company, a vice-president who had graduated from the same university as I, had always been friendly to me. When we moved to our second plant, he found out what I'd done and came over to have a friendly visit with me. When he saw the molding machines lined up nicely, he remarked, "Jerry would die to have such a factory."

A few months later, I received a letter from Mr. Stewart asking me if I could help him find some aluminum materials.

I called and told him I was in plastics and knew nothing about buying aluminum. I'm sure he already knew that, as my vice-president friend must have already told him. I guessed he wanted to open communication with me, but I did not pick up on the invitation, as I would not have felt proud to show him our plant that was still small and old.

Basically, I never wished to show what I had done to anyone who had belittled me. Such a gesture would seem I was saying, "Hey, now you see? I showed you." That was never necessary.

One man who really hurt my feelings was the dean of the Engineering Department at the Chinese university. Although he never taught me in any class, I was sure he knew I didn't have good grades. One day, when I was in his office for something, I remarked that I wanted to go to the United States to study business administration. He must have thought I was just dreaming. I could almost feel him thinking, "What a fool! How can he go to the United States?"

He said to me, "You don't have to go to America. You can get books and read them yourself here."

I didn't respond. Then he looked at me disrespectfully and asked, "Do you think you want to be a professor?" What he meant was that I could never qualify for such an exalted position.

I did not say anything; I just left his office. He certainly had insulted me a great deal, particularly since I was sensitive about my poor performance in the Mechanical Engineering Department. Of course, he didn't know I had never wanted to study engineering in the first place.

Confucius said: "Bo Yi did not nurse old grudges, so others didn't have ill feeling toward him."

My dean hurt my feelings deeply, when he implied that I could never be qualified to be a professor. However, I resolved not to take his insult too seriously. I had less worry without holding a grudge.

On the way back to my dormitory, I began to think how merciless the man could be. I had never respected him as a person, because I believed that he adhered to no principles. I feel that everyone should have a moral code, something they would never do, such as "I will never kill" or "I will never steal." People can hold such ethics easily, but many are willing to fudge. They may decide cheating on their taxes is not really stealing, for example. Many might find it difficult to keep to a principle like, "I will honestly serve my country." To satisfy their ego, such persons would do anything to win a government office.

I was reminded of a story: A judge sentenced a thief to prison. The thief said to the judge, "Your Honor, if you let me go I'll give you one thousand dollars." The judge yelled, "Stop! I must send you to prison." The thief again said, "How about one million dollars?" The judge hollered, "Guards! Take him away quickly. It's getting dangerous."

To hold to a principle requires a strong personality. Some people enjoy political activities and join the government to serve the public, even to contribute to society. This is commendable. Others want to get rich through public service, and that is foolish. They should go into business!

9

Buying the Second Plant

"Knowing your opponent and knowing yourself, you can go into a hundred battles and never be defeated."

—Sunzi's *Art of War*

When we outgrew our rented plant in 1973, we had waited until we had to add more molding machines before starting to look for a larger facility to buy. Because Chicago had many buildings of the size we needed, we spent only a little over a year to find a suitable one. Years passed, and by 1982, we again outgrew our space. While looking for a much larger building, we subcontracted extra work to smaller qualified molding shops.

The situation between the city and the suburbs had not changed too much, and we decided that we still wanted to stay in Chicago. The city had established an Economic Development Commission, which issued revenue bonds for some industries that wanted to stay in the city. Getting a revenue bond to finance a building at much lower interest rate would be a big advantage.

I asked Mr. Goldman, the industrial real-estate broker who had bought our first building, to look for a larger facility for us. The requirements were similar, but the size had to be four or five times larger. After about three months, he had come up with practically nothing.

The task turned out to be truly difficult, as only a limited number of buildings of the size we needed were available. I began to feel the pressure and engaged two more brokers. They took me all over the city and showed me many large buildings, but none was suitable. Then, I notified more brokers and began to feel that all the industrial property brokers were working for me. After about a year, I knew of more industrial properties than any one of those brokers.

Finally, I saw a For Sale sign on a building situated north of our current plant and looked at it. The building was not perfect, but we could get by with it. After several visits, the owner and I reached an agreement and shook hands. He asked me to draw up a contract, and I agreed. My attorney finished the contract based on our verbal understanding, and I gave copies of the contract to the building owner to sign, but he came up with all kinds of excuses not to sign.

After two months, I caught him on the phone and said, "If you do not want to sell your building, it's perfectly all right, but tell me, so I can look for others. Don't keep me hanging like this."

He suggested we have lunch to talk about it. I thought he might want to make some changes to the contract, so I agreed. During the lunch, he did not bring up any discussion concerning the contract. After the lunch, he would not offer to pay the bill, and I had to pay it. Furthermore, he still didn't tell me if he'd changed his mind about selling the building. Once he had gotten a free lunch from me, I never heard from him again. What a sucker I was, and all because I was anxious to buy a building.

Two years passed, and by 1984, our plant had become so congested, we had to use the parking lot to arrange inventories. When the forklift came to the lot, we had to park our cars on the street. Out of the blue, a broker called and told me he had found a large, beautiful building just put up for sale. I went over right away.

The building was not far from our current plant, fairly new, and well built. It had a one-hundred-thousand-square-foot factory, and six thousand square feet of office space, plus an empty lot of forty thousand square feet in the back. Everything was right except for one feature: The beams and ceiling were made of laminated wood. With our plastic-molding operation handling high-temperature materials, the wood ceiling would be a fire hazard.

I telephoned the fire chief of the village where I lived and asked him for advice about the ceiling. He told me without hesitation that a wooden ceiling was actually the best ceiling for industries. If it caught fire, it would burn a large hole in a very short time. The heat would travel up and out through the hole, and the fire would spread slowly. The damage would thus be limited to one area of the building. If the ceiling were made of steel frame, the heat would be kept inside the building. When the steel melted, the whole building would collapse at once.

After gaining this information from the fire chief, I made an offer to the building owner through the broker. Five weeks went by, and the broker could not conclude the deal.

Facing the uncertainty of not being able to buy the building was not healthy. Since I had been looking at various industrial buildings for nearly three years, I had a pretty good idea about a fair price for this building. The company that owned the building was having trouble with its union. The owner wanted to move to a far away northern town in order to get rid of the union. Therefore, he was eager to sell and was asking a reasonable price. I called my broker.

"You have not been able to make much progress with this building," I said. "Let me negotiate with the owner. I'll let you know when a deal is made. You can spend your time and energy on something else. You and I will split the five percent commission." He agreed.

I engaged an appraiser to evaluate the building. After he gave me the figure, I called the owner and said, "My broker has not been able to help us with regard to your building. I would like to invite you to lunch, we can talk about it, just you and me."

"Good idea," he agreed.

"What food would you like to eat?" I asked him.

"I like Chinese food," he told me. I suggested we meet at a nice Chinese restaurant.

During the lunch, I said, "I will tell you frankly that I need a large building badly. I also know you are under pressure to sell your building. I heard your union contract is coming up soon, and you have to move fast. Why don't we try to agree on a price right now?"

He started to set the stage. "John, I like your frankness. You know our asking price is a very good one."

"Your price is not out of line," I agreed. "I have a figure that I think is very fair, and we both can be happy about it." I told him my offer.

He swallowed the food in his mouth and sipped some water from the glass. He looked at me for a moment and then said, "It's a deal."

We shook hands. The whole negotiation took about ten minutes.

We exchanged our attorneys' names and telephone numbers.

Sunzi wrote: "In war, we value victory, not long campaign."

A few days later, my broker came in with another broker who some time before had shown me some buildings. Apparently they were friends. The unsuccessful broker shook my hand and said, "Congratulations. You have bought a very nice building."

"Thank you," I said.

"You know I have worked very hard for you all this time," he said. "I think I deserve a share of the commission for this building deal."

I couldn't believe my ears. I thought for a moment, "Is this man crazy? How can he try to rob someone he knows?"

I said to him, "What are you talking about? What did you have to do with this building?"

He insisted on a share of the commission until I became so angry, I told him to get out of my office. Eventually, he left. I turned to my broker and asked, "What's matter with this guy? Is he sick?"

"You can't blame him for trying," my broker said, and shrugged.

Over the years, Chicago had been losing industry for various reasons, so City Hall had been trying hard to hold on to what it had and to encourage outsiders to settle in the city. We applied for the low-interest revenue bonds for the building we intended to buy. With the help of corporate and bond attorneys, I worked with the Economic Development Commission for a few months, and finally we were approved.

But we ran into a problem: our bank was too small to handle the whole revenue bond. It could buy only half of the bond, and we had to find another bank for the other half.

Our bank recommended a bond broker who was working for another financial institution, and he was able to negotiate a very advantageous deal for his employers. I, now, wish I'd tried myself to find another bank to buy the other half of the revenue bond, without using broker and incurring a broker's fee. But the real lesson I learned was that a company should not use a bank too small to handle large loans for expansion.

My accountant recommended I buy the building myself and rent it to my company. This was one way to take some money out of the company in the form of rent and put the money into personal assets. Most of the time, the tax rate for individuals is lower than for businesses.

Separating the building and the business had many advantages. If I ever had to sell the business, I could keep the building, if I wanted to and vice-versa. I would also have more flexibility in managing assets. So that was what we did, and, before long, the purchasing process had been completed.

The building, a large empty shell, had been built by an electric company to serve as its distribution center in the Chicago area. We laid out molding room, tool room, quality-control room, and lunchroom. All the doors to these rooms were located close to one another, so people would find it easy to visit each other and to communicate.

After the machinery, water system, and resin-handling system had been installed, everybody was excited and felt a sense of success. Some friends, customers, and suppliers came by to see our new building and congratulate us. Some, of course, were more sincere than others.

An engineer from my friend's ski equipment company came to town and stopped by to say hello. I took him to lunch. While we were eating, he said, "John, I hope you don't mind if I ask you this: This building needs a lot of money. How can you afford to pay for all this?"

I smiled. "I don't have to pay. The bank pays, and the bank owns." We both laughed.

A man I'd been friend with for twenty years came to my office to discuss a project. He had been recommending and selling modern industrial products to us for many years. We had invited him and his wife to our annual company Christmas party ever since we'd started the event.

On the way to the restaurant, he said, "This project requires a lot of money. How do you finance it?"

"I got a revenue bond from the city," I answered.

"What's the interest rate?" he asked.

"Very low."

"How much?" he insisted.

I told him the approximate rate. Upon hearing it, his neck turned red, and the color spread until it covered his whole face. "All you immigrants! You get everything!" he thundered.

Chinese proverb: "True character is revealed in moments of extreme anger."

I did not respond. Never would I have suspected he harbored so much bitterness against immigrants. He himself was only the third generation of a German immigrant.

He had just built a new office in a western suburb on a large tract of valuable land situated near expressways and toll ways. The local government would not need to offer any incentive to attract people to such an area and, of course, he would have to pay a higher interest rate to the bank. Had he chosen to locate his business in Chicago, he could have gotten a revenue bond. Applicants did not have to be immigrants to get a revenue bond.

During lunch, we didn't mention immigrants or revenue bonds. I was sure he felt regretful to have shown his true colors like that. I was sorry to know that during all those years he'd thought of me different.

This immigrant didn't mind working in the Chicago environment, while the third generation man wanted to breathe fresher air where he worked. He had said immigrants get all the benefits. He probably felt I had surpassed him by buying such a large plant; but I was in a mass-production business, while he marketed industrial equipment. Naturally, he did not need a large plant. Anyway, he must have had a fixed opinion about the aggressiveness of first-generation immigrants who had to struggle to survive, just like his grandfather had, not too long before. I found I felt sorry for him.

Confucius said: "If you are tolerant, you will win over many."

We still do business with his company, as long as it renders good service. But when I got home that afternoon, I crossed his name off our Christmas party guest list.

Having moved to a much larger and more modern facility, the staff felt somewhat displaced and uneasy. Suddenly, accidents began to happen.

My office manager, Geri, told me, "We haven't had a single accident in a very long time, I don't even remember how long! But since we moved in two weeks ago, two guys have cut their fingers. This morning, Virginia slipped and fell in the parking lot. If that's not a jinx, what is it?"

"Coincidences," I told her. "Accidents happen sometimes, particularly when the surroundings change and people aren't used to the new environment. The so-called jinx exists only in your own mind. A curse is like a rumor. Ignore it, and it eventually dies out."

After a couple of months passed with no further mishaps, Geri let go of her fears.

About a year later, some kids started to build a tree house on a tree along the railroad tracks near our parking lot border. When we'd first moved in, some youngsters had thrown rocks at our windows or at our cars, while they walked along the tracks, but by the time construction started on the tree house, nobody was bothering us.

To be friendly, I gave the kids several pieces of lumber, for which they thanked me. Unfortunately, an accident happened: A boy fell out of the tree house and landed on the cement border of our parking lot. He was hurt pretty badly.

Everybody was sued, the railroad company, the lumberyard that gave the boys the lumber, and Magenta. The suit was settled out of court, with our insurance company paying five thousand dollars to the boy's family. If this accident had happened one year before, Geri would have sworn it had been the biggest jinx.

Jinx or no jinx, just around this time the second daughter of my distant cousin came to Chicago to join her younger sister. She brought me the true story of what happened to my parents during the revolution.

In the late 1940s, after the Japanese lost the war and the communists took over the central government, the wave of revolution reached our town. Since my grandfather had bought land for his sons, my family became a target of the revolt, and our land was distributed to the farmers.

Some landowners were paraded in the street like criminals; others were killed. But since our family had been kind to the townspeople, they let my parents escape during the night.

A distant uncle had carried my mother from our house to his and offered to let my parents stay with them during the crisis. He told my parents, "If there is food for us, there will be for you."

But my parents preferred to go to Beijing to live with my brother, so this uncle accompanied them to Beijing. There they found that my brother was having trouble with his wife and did not have space for my parents anyway, so my parents settled at another uncle's place, the younger brother of the hometown uncle who had helped my parents since the trouble started.

This younger uncle managed a coal yard in Beijing. He made one room available for my parents. But the person who helped my parents the most in daily life during their darkest days was Jun, the elder daughter of my hometown uncle. She was helping the Beijing uncle at the time. When her family had something special to eat, she often brought some of the food to my parents.

My parents suffered a great deal until the early 1950s, when I was able to begin sending money to them. Unfortunately, most of these people had passed away by the time China opened communication with the West in 1979, when I was able to visit Beijing.

In the mid 1980s, I found out through a relative that the wife of the uncle who had carried my mother was still living in our hometown. I immediately sent money to her to show my appreciation. Later my relative told me that this old lady had said to him, "I could never dream of using the fat baby's money." Family members had nicknamed me "fat baby", because I was a very round infant.

In the early 1990s, my cousin Jun caught a chronic illness, and I have helped her with all her medical expenses ever since. I hope I have paid her back for her kindness toward my parents.

10

Loyalty

"Treat people with honesty; gain others' heart with your own heart."

—Chinese proverb

My first employee, Daniel, the foreman, and later, the superintendent of the plant, was a hardworking man, conscientious, loyal, and particularly good with his hands. He joined me when I started my business with so little capital, and I always felt that anyone who would take a chance on me like that deserved my loyalty.

Daniel personally unloaded thousands of pounds of resins with his arms and shoulders. He managed the plant well when we had three to five molding machines and the quality requirements from customers were not so strict.

When we had more machines and more employees, however, he began to show signs of stress. Whenever we had trouble in the plant, such as a machine breakdown, operator no-show, or electricity outage, he became disturbed and often angry. I could sense that he was near the limit of his capacity.

I began to teach him positive attitude, well explained by Napoleon Hill and W. Clement Stone in their book *Success through a Positive Mental Attitude.* I told Daniel to think positively about our ability to solve problems, and to take the stance of never giving up. But I couldn't get him to understand what positivity really meant.

One day, Daniel said to me, "John, you always say to have a positive mental attitude. I have tried very hard. Driving to work this morning, I kept telling myself to think positively, and there would be no trouble in the plant today. We would get all the machines started without a problem. You know what happened?"

He paused, and I looked at him attentively, listening. "The moment I got to the plant," he continued, "I saw one machine down. The third-shift guy had screwed it up. One girl has not shown up yet. And one job is finishing, and I have to make another mold change. All my positive thinking on the way here this morning meant nothing, damn it!"

I had gone over all this with him before, but obviously he needed to hear it again. I quietly and patiently said, "Thinking positively does not prevent problems from happening. Taking a positive attitude means that we don't let troubles and problems get us down, that we don't give up trying to solve them, or prevent them from recurring in the future."

He turned around and went to work.

Hmmm, I thought: "Even Confucius isn't helping this time."

Confucius said: "If on showing someone one corner, he does not come back with the other three, I will not repeat the lesson."

I came up with the idea that the basic Dale Carnegie course might do him some good. I sent him and our tool room foreman to the Carnegie Management seminar. When they had finished the course, I asked them to summarize for a group of foremen and staff members what they had learned at the seminar.

Our tool room foreman was an intelligent fellow and rather shy. He related a couple of points that had impressed him the most at the seminar. When our superintendent came to the front of the group, he brought with him a reference book used in the seminar. He said what he thought was important had been written in two paragraphs in the book, which he read aloud, then sat down.

He seemed to have chosen the important parts of the book to read, but he didn't tell us the essence in his own words. I really did not know what Daniel had learned at the seminar, but I felt sure that it hadn't done him any harm.

Before long, I reached the conclusion that he might be able to oversee a routine that was already up and running, but definitely could not move up to new technology, modern management concepts, new communications and quality control systems, rules, procedures, and so on.

Once, I asked him, "We have rejects again?"

He answered, "John, we produce many millions of parts. A few rejects mean practically nothing. What do they expect?"

Daniel could never understand that times had changed, and one defective part was one too many. I didn't argue or explain, however; I'd tried that before without success.

When we moved to our third plant, we invested in automation, and I replaced Daniel with a young man and changed the title from superintendent to plant manager. Originally, maintenance had been taken care of by the plant manager, but since Daniel was handy and knew about the building, I put him in charge of building maintenance and the related areas, such as heating, cooling, lighting, and landscaping. I created the position just for him, did not mention his title, and didn't reduce his salary.

Although not a highly skilled job, maintenance involved more than just replacing light bulbs; it actually required planning, establishing, and keeping maintenance programs and preventing emergencies. For instance, he had to set up a schedule to inspect the roof and fix it before it leaked, but he did nothing of the sort. When we had no building problem, he just walked around.

One day, I called him to my office and told him that to be a maintenance boss, he had to establish preventive procedures for all systems, not just wait for trouble to happen. He listened but made no response. I guessed he was feeling kind of depressed and lost.

I thought of another idea. I called him to my office again and said, "I remember your telling me that you have a friend who was thinking of opening a hardware store. You have a lot of money in the profit-sharing fund. Why don't you put up some money and open a hardware store with him as a partner?"

He listened but again said nothing.

I continued. "You would need only a part of your money. Also, in any business, the first few months are critical, I'll pay you six months' salary after you leave and have our attorney help you on legal matters at the company's expense. Why don't you talk to your wife about this idea?"

Finally, he answered, "I'll think about it."

A few weeks passed, and he told me nothing. One day, I met him at the plant entrance and said, "I have not heard from you. I presume you do not want to go into the hardware business."

"I don't think I want to go into any business," he answered in a low voice.

Because we had dealt with too many emergencies in maintenance and Daniel did not show any indication of leaving the company, I had no choice but to reduce his responsibility to that of a maintenance man working under the plant manager. I still did not cut his salary.

As I tried to think of the solution for this man, I focused on the basic idea of Confucian philosophy, which is benevolence and having an upright heart. I remembered that years before, I had attended a seminar on personnel management. The speaker brought up the problem of an old employee who could not advance as the company progressed. He called such a man an "Old Charlie." He said the only way to deal with such a problem was to fire him.

I did not agree. One person's pay cannot break a company. When a person has been loyal to the company for many years, how can anyone have the heart to put him out in the street? Now, we had an Old Charlie, and I kept him. Several times he made me so angry that I could have fired him on the spot, but didn't. Deep in my heart I felt sorry for him. That he didn't have Einstein's brain was not his fault.

The other employees knew about Daniel's poor performance with high pay because he was an old, loyal employee. This example made everybody else feel more secure and tend to be more loyal to the company.

One time, a toolmaker made a silly mistake, and our tool chief became furious, yelling, "You're so stupid!"

After he cooled down a bit, I said to him, "Don't be so angry. The man is dumb, but can he help it? His parents did not give him a smart head. That's out of his control. Think how lucky you are, to have intelligence. What did you do to deserve such a valuable gift from your parents? Nothing. Maybe you worked harder in school and acquired more knowledge, but that's because you were already smart and lucky enough to attend a good school. I say we should feel sorry for him."

He was silent for a moment, then said, "Well, if you look at it that way."

"To be honest, I've gotten angry many times, because somebody did something stupid," I said frankly. "But we are all human. The world needs all kinds of people. Some work with their hands and others with their heads."

Mencius said: "People should use loyalty as the foundation for doing things."

With these thoughts in mind, I began to think of the good things our Old Charlie had done. During the first few years in business, he had helped us survive and, in fact, to grow. He never intentionally did anything bad. As a maintenance man, he had done a pretty good job.

With the superintendent's salary, he could save extra money each year. In a few years he would reach retirement age. At that time, he would have a large sum of profit-sharing money. Since he was a conservative person, I predicted he would keep his money safe for life.

As I was from an old country where people historically have emphasized loyalty, it came naturally to me to be loyal to my employees. This man, our first employee, certainly deserved our respectful treatment.

Chinese proverb: "Well starts and well ends."

In the course of doing business, my relationships with certain people grew from professional to friendly. For example, my banker, Byron O'Connor, was an exceptionally kind man and became one of my best friends. When I applied for the government guaranteed loan and got so frustrated with the man at the agency, Byron comforted me by saying, "We just ran into a bad guy, that's all. It could happen to anybody."

Then, I told myself that the situation might be meant to test my perseverance. I remembered, a couple of times, during our first year in business, when I had to call Byron and ask him for some cash to meet our payroll. When I arrived at the bank, he always had a five thousand dollars check ready for me.

A few years later, the bank president passed away, the vice-president retired, and the new management was made up of a group of untrustworthy people coming from a large bank in Chicago. They forced my friend out, and he got a job at another bank. After a few months, I moved our account to his new bank.

Byron was not happy in this new situation, after a couple of years, he moved to a bank just like his old one, small, with a family atmosphere, and I moved our account to his bank right away. At that time, our account was not small anymore.

I noticed that in the course of all this upheaval, Byron's weight had shot up. The president of his old bank had tried to persuade him to lose weight, but Byron had not taken the request seriously. Now, I thought the matter had become urgent.

I called him on the phone and said, "Byron, this time I have to be firm. I think you'll have to reduce if you want to live a long time. I'm your friend, and I do not want to lose you. Go to your doctor right away for a checkup and ask him to recommend a weight-reduction program. I will pay for all your reducing expenses."

"Thank you very much," he said. "You don't have to pay for my expenses. I promise you I will do it. I'll call my doctor right away."

He lost one hundred pounds in about a year. I'm so glad he did; I would miss him as a friend, if anything happened to him.

A feeling of loyalty grew within me for several of my customers. Jim Adams, for example, had helped us to become an important supplier for his corporation in Kentucky. While the corporation was doing its own molding, Mr. Adams received a super deal from his company and retired at an early age. To show our loyalty and respect, I invited him to come watch our daily operations for a few days and tell us what improvements we should make.

The next year, I asked him to be our representative in the Kentucky area to sell plastic custom molding. Since he had known us so long and so well, he agreed to help. Not long after he joined us, the Kentucky corporation gave up self-molding and offered us a chance to work for them again. Most the people there respected our representative, therefore, he did not have to work too hard to persuade them to use Magenta. The situation was rewarding for everyone concerned.

After a couple of years, at the annual Christmas party, Mr. Adams took me to a quiet corner and asked, "John, is it all right that I have made so much money from your company?" He was serious.

I smiled and responded, "Why, that's your commission! You earned it. I hope you'll make more, because that would mean we'll make more, too."

He repeated, "I just thought it was too much. We are doing unexpectedly well."

"And that's good," I said, then escorted him to the buffet table. I closed the discussion with an appreciation of what a wholesome gentleman he is!

We not only trusted our other friends, such as attorneys, accountants, consulting engineers, and so on, but also showed them loyalty. In return, they provided excellent service and were also loyal to us.

Years ago, corporations tried to keep their employees for life, particularly in Japan. When I visited a plastic molding machine factory there in the 1970s, one of the two fellows who accompanied me had just finished college. He told me that he had three companies to choose from for his career. All were near his home. Finally, he decided on the machine company that already had a plan for him to work for life.

Sadly, loyalty has been lost in the corporate world in recent years. In order to meet global competition, corporations worldwide have cut costs by downsizing, and loyalty has gone down the drain. In order to protect themselves, employees try to earn as much as they can in the shortest time where the pay is the highest.

Magenta is relatively small and can try to nurture loyalty between the company and employees. We have maintained a family atmosphere to encourage loyalty, and whenever possible have promoted employees from within our organization. Over the years, we promoted a good number of employees to responsible positions. All our setup men and foremen and some managers were promoted from the position of floor boy.

Confucius said: "Promote the good and the talented."

The leader of the setup men had been with us for over fifteen years. He had come from Poland as a young fellow. Another young man came on as a floor boy at the age of nineteen, just graduated from high school. In a few years he became a foreman. He worked briefly as the superintendent of our plant and settled down to be our production-planning manager.

Our purchasing manager also started as a floor boy. He was promoted to overseeing shipping, receiving, and inventories. When we discovered another young man capable of handling shipping and receiving work, we moved this man up to purchasing manager.

Our customer-service manager started with us as an estimator, assisting salesmen, fresh from college over twenty-five years ago. Our assistant plant manager whose mother is Geri, our retired office manager, was promoted from the position of floor boy.

Our plant manager, a young and quiet fellow, came as a floor boy and later, became a foreman. Throughout this period he worked the third shift, from midnight to eight in the morning. Consequently, he rarely had the opportunity to be in contact with management people, particularly when his shift had no problem. As a result, management did not notice his capability until he was transferred to the day shift as assistant plant manager. A few years ago, we hired a plant manager from outside, but his performance did not quite meet our expectations. When he left, we made this assistant manager our plant manager right away. He proved to be a very innovative boss.

Among all the personnel promotions, one of the most rewarding is our new product manager, Rich. While he worked for us as our most knowledgeable mold repairman, he had a fine machine shop in the basement of his house. He operated his shop in his spare time as a machinist contractor, producing unparalleled precision machine work. He could fix antique cars and owned a few himself as a hobby. He also played musical instruments for his own enjoyment.

These various interests did not prevent him from being the most reliable and honest man I have ever known. If Rich told us that he had worked on a company project at his basement machine shop during the weekend for four hours, we trusted him and paid him. He probably had worked five hours and spent some time drinking coffee.

However, he had personal problems. As a child he helped his father moving pianos and at the age of ten hurt his back. His mother was an alcoholic. His German parents treated him so cruelly that, later in life, he thought everyone in the world was cruel and untrustworthy.

When our tool chief passed away, our tool-repair expert had worked for us for over ten years. I called him to my office and said, "Rich, I want you to be our tool chief and move into his office. You will manage the technical side of the tool room. Personnel problems and job assignments will be the tool room working foreman's responsibility."

His answer was fast and straightforward. "No. I belong to the bench. I do not belong in an office. I don't feel good if I don't wear this apron."

"Think it over," I told him quietly. "You will not be bothered by the daily tool room routines. Primarily, you will handle new mold designs and experimental molds. You will give technical advice, if the foreman asks."

"I don't have those degrees. I'm a toolmaker," he repeated.

"I know you'll do a good job as tool chief, or whatever we'll call you," I said to him. "Otherwise, I wouldn't ask you to do it. Think it over for a few days."

After more persuasion, he agreed to move into the chief's office; otherwise, he could not use the drafting table. He laid out two conditions. One was that he would still maintain a working bench in the tool room, and the other, he would not have a big title.

Of course, Rich could have his bench, and for the time being, I didn't have to give him any title.

At first, he checked all new mold designs and mold revisions before orders for mold works could be released. Later on, as we paid more attention to new products, he practically turned into a new-product design and development man. When we introduced him to visitors, we called him the new product manager, and he did not object.

Rich made many valuable contributions to new products. Since he knew molds and molding, he was more practical in mold design conception than other mold design engineers. Sometimes, he offered ideas to make a product easier to mold. Although his suggestions did not always add features to the patent of invention, we made him a coinventor and had his name printed on patent certificates. When he did add a feature to an invention, we made him one of the inventors and hung up a plaque with his name, on the wall of the conference room.

With all these honors, he finally settled down in his office and seemed comfortable.

All our quality-control inspectors were promoted from machine operators. Even our first quality-control manager had been a floor boy. He was a college graduate from a Middle Eastern country and a very hard worker. Often, when we had quality problems during the third shift, he would get up in the middle of his sleep and come to the plant to help. As he did not have quality-control knowledge, we sent him to the university part-time for several years to take courses on quality control.

His contribution was limited by his lack of leadership skills. He did not know how to manage people and how to schedule the work. Although he was a hard worker, eventually our president replaced him with a man who had a quality-control degree and experience with a modern industrial corporation.

We offered him an engineer position, but he refused and quit. We knew he was not the type of person who would sue the company, but after many months he sued us for discrimination against a foreign minority; somebody undoubtedly had advised him to do so. After several months of negotiation with our insurance company, they settled for a reasonable compensation. But he never signed a paper releasing the company from further responsibility and never cashed the settlement check.

The mistake I made was being too impressed by his hard work and ignoring his lack of ability to manage. It seemed that he hadn't learned much about quality-control systems at the university, either. The fact that he didn't take the compensation and, instead, just disappeared might be due to the loyalty I had shown him in the early years.

Aside from this single failure, all our promotions were successful and rewarding. The employees we promoted seemingly planned to stay with us for life. Even those who were not promoted to take on more responsibilities have been advanced in wages and bonuses, with a larger share of the profit-sharing fund. Most of these people have also been with us for many years.

If we want employees to be loyal to us, we have to be loyal to them first. Loyalty is a long-term commitment. One cannot be loyal to someone just once. Instead, one has to commit his loyalty from the beginning to the end. I had been always loyal to my employees, and the indication of their loyalty to me is that so many have stayed with me for life.

11

Abusing the Law

"Good will be requited with good, evil requited with evil."

—Chinese proverb

As Magenta slowly became a bigger operation, we began thinking about intangible matters such as management and policies. Our first priority was to set up some guidelines for hiring.

Entrepreneurs must never forget, even for a minute, that it is easy to hire but awfully difficult to fire. When I interviewed a job applicant, this question always floated in my mind: Will this person give me trouble in the future, if we are not on good terms?

Because of this concern, I often hired a person based on their honest face rather than an indication of high capability.

Due to the difficulty of firing, particularly in regard to friends or relatives, I set up our one guideline: When filling a position, follow normal hiring procedures through personnel agencies, newspaper advertisements, or recommendations, and preferably do not hire relatives or friends of family. We also preferred not to have a husband and wife, brother and sister, mother and son, and so forth working with us at the same time.

I turned down the son of one of our stockholders and the brother of a friend of my wife's from her church. One of my best friends asked if I would let his son do some legal work for me when he graduated from law school, and I refused because we already had a corporate lawyer. All my refusals made the people unhappy at the time, but none of them became an enemy.

I brought a second cousin to the United States from China to go to college. I planned to let him gain experience in our company after he finished school, but he turned out to be a poor student and a liar. Needless to say, I abandoned my plan. Eventually, my cousin was expelled by the school and went to work in a Chinese restaurant.

Something very wonderful came about as a result of my offer to help the boy, however. When I took him to register at the university, a young Chinese lady named Helen Loo was helping foreign students. I asked her to look after my cousin, and she did.

A couple of years after she received her master's degree in accounting, I helped her gain a position in my accountant's office, but she didn't stay long. Some time later, she called and asked my advice about a business venture she and her girl-friend were considering. I invited them to lunch and discussed their concept with them.

Three years passed, and suddenly Helen phoned and told me she was going back to China. She just wanted to say goodbye, and see if she might be able to do something for me over there.

I wanted to ask her to buy a book for me in China, so I invited her to a fare-well lunch. During the meal, Helen told me she had just passed the CPA examination, and then said, "You look tired. Are you sick?"

I told her my wife had passed away a few months before. I added, "I guess I am kind of tired."

She expressed her condolences.

After a couple of months, Helen changed her mind, returned to the U.S., and became a reporter for a Chinese newspaper. About eight months later, we got married. Two years later, in 1985, our son, Jordan, was born, a healthy and good-looking boy.

Although Helen had no opportunity to help in the company, all departments were being operated by trained personnel, she greatly relieved my pressure at home by managing our money matters, shopping, paying bills, and researching and discussing investments.

The guideline of not hiring friends and relatives eliminated only a few person-nel who might have caused trouble. The main challenge continued to be deter-mining who was honest and who was not.

Once, a man came in to apply for a mold setup job in response to our newspa-per advertisement. He said he had worked in a plastic molding shop and done mechanical work in Puerto Rico. He was in his thirties, healthy, and full of stam-ina. I thought, if he had a little experience in plastic molding, we would be able to train him.

After some questions and answers, I told him, "I will give you a chance. If you can prove you can do the job within the trial period of two months, you will be permanently hired and receive a ten cents per hour raise. If, by my judgment, you cannot do the job, you will have to leave, and I do not have to tell you the reason. Do you understand, and do you agree?"

"Yes," he answered.

After one month, we reached the conclusion that this man had never worked in plastic molding shop, or on any mechanical jobs. He tried hard, but we didn't have time to train a beginner. I called him to my office and told him he'd lied about his plastic molding experience, and we would have to let him go. I suggested he start looking for another job.

Hearing this, he instantly became furious. "I know it's all that son-of-a-bitch foreman. He doesn't like me," he said angrily. "If you fire me, I'll follow him to his house after work. I'll set fire to his house and cut his tires."

Uh oh, we are in trouble, I thought. But keep cool. I told him quietly, "You agreed that within two months, I could let you go without telling you the reason."

"Yes. But I want to stay here," he said. "I am a Puerto Rican. Nobody wants me."

"If you are worrying about finding a job, I'll help you by giving you more time," I said. "I'll pay you two weeks extra pay. You should be able to find a job then."

But with a scowl he raised his right fist, pounded on my desk, and yelled, "Two weeks pay?"

"What else do you think you deserve?" I asked.

"I want to stay here," he answered.

"Do you think I dare to have you here after you have behaved like this?" I asked.

He answered loudly, "I'm going to burn your house too."

I kept silent for a few moments, and he stood quietly in front of my desk. When he had cooled off somewhat, I bargained with him and settled for one month extra pay based on a ten-cents raise. Geri gave him a check in minutes, and he left.

This guy certainly had a bad temper. How could we know he was this kind of person during the interview? In the future, I resolved to spend more time checking the references the applicant provided. If we had found out that he had never worked in plastic shop in the beginning, we would not have hired him and had this kind of trouble.

Confucius said: "Human beings are similar in their basic nature, but vary widely due to different environments."

This case showed us that firing an employee is difficult, even with cause. When the company and employee have a good relationship, to fire is still hard.

One time, we hired a young girl, well mannered, good-natured, and pleasant. She didn't know office work, but we thought she could learn. However, before the two-month trial period ended, we concluded that office work was not for her and advised her to seek something else she might find more interesting and rewarding.

Upon hearing this bad news, she cried.

"Shirley, this is not the end of the world," I said. "You are young. I am sure you can find some work you will really enjoy doing."

She responded immediately, "But I like it here!"

"Your future is not in an office of a small factory," I said. "You might like to do sales. Come, I will drive you home since your mother is at work."

She slowly regained her composure.

"Look, it is already lunch time," I said. "I'll take you to lunch on the way."

We went to an Italian restaurant where we often invited visitors to lunch. The moment we walked in, the owner came over with a big smile.

"Hello, sir! This way, please."

He ushered us to a small private room, one of only two in the restaurant.

I laughed and said, "We don't have to sit here. This is not hanky-panky. This is business."

Our young lady finally laughed. Later, I heard she was working as a salesgirl at a Bakery where her mother worked.

Chinese proverb: "In a melon field don't tie your shoelace, and in a fruit orchard do not fix your hat"—in other words, do not behave in a way that can arouse suspicion.

Some might say that I shouldn't have taken the young secretary to lunch, because it could appear suspicious. But I would do it again, because it made her happier, and I had nothing to worry about, when my conscience was clear.

Judging character accurately is a very difficult skill to acquire. People who have experience dealing with many different types usually can assess character better than those who have interacted with fewer people. Some professionals claim they have accurate ways to assess a job applicant's character. They have created questionnaires, and the answers can be interpreted, analyzed, and used to define the integrity of the applicant. But the process is not totally reliable.

Sometimes, however, I have found we can draw conclusions or make predictions from what we can see. For instance, if a person walks slowly, he most likely has little drive and is not apt to accomplish much. This person might not be punctual. On the other hand, a person who walks too fast tends to be nervous. A person who walks straight with his head up and with an erect posture is likely to be a good worker.

From these observations, we did employ walking as one criterion in our interviews. If an applicant walked in slowly and, particularly, walked out slowly also, we usually did not hire the person. Although this observation was not scientific enough to be totally reliable, we still liked to use it as a guideline.

When we hired a worker, we tried to choose people who would be capable of taking on more responsibilities in the future. We always promoted qualified women to become quality-control personnel, whom we called inspectors. This way we offered women opportunities for advancement.

Unskilled young men, mostly fresh from high school, we hired as floor boys. During the interview we always asked ourselves if this boy could be promoted to a foreman one day and do a good job. Our plant manager had been promoted from the position of floor boy. Promotion potential was included on our list of employee guidelines.

Although we were sincerely loyal to our employees, we still had problems with some of them and settled many minor employee disputes.

For instance, one day two female employees came into my office, both crying. One was an African-American and the other white. One accused the other of using bad language and fighting. Apparently, the foreman hadn't been there, when the dispute started.

I stood up from my chair and walked to the door to meet them. "I can see this is quite serious," I said, "but right now, I'm just too busy. Both of you go home today. Tomorrow morning come to me, and we'll see who was right and who was wrong."

They stopped crying and left my office without a word

Chinese proverb: "Cannot clap with one hand."

The next morning, I went to the plant and found them working peacefully. I smiled and asked, "Sue, you feel good today?"

"Yes," she answered in a very low voice.

I walked to the other disputant and said, "Joyce, you feel all right?"

"Yeah," she answered.

I said, "Good," and walked away. Letting them wait till the next morning to talk about the problem had been the best way to cool them off. Now, that they were past their anger, everything was back to normal.

Sunzi wrote: "Anger can cease."

Fighting and arguing between workers was a violation of the company rule. Disputes were a common occurrence, however, and not considered a serious violation.

Confucius said: "Be lenient toward minor offenses

These problems were truly small compared with the cases of people abusing the law. We never violated any discrimination law in practice or in spirit, but we were defrauded a few times by dishonest employees using legal loopholes.

For example, the law forbids companies to refuse to hire people, just because they have diabetes or other chronic illness. Therefore, during an interview, we do not ask the applicant if he or she has any chronic medical conditions. If the interviewer asks and the applicant answers yes, and for whatever reason the company does not hire the person, he can sue and claim that the company did not hire him because of his illness. To prove that the company had good cause for not hiring the person is very difficult.

We once hired an intelligent-looking young fellow as a floor boy. After he came to work, we learned he had diabetes. We told him, "Diabetes is serious. Everything will be okay if you take care of yourself and listen to your doctor." He said he would. Then, we found out he also had the habit of drinking alcohol, a dangerous combination. We warned him that he should not drink, and he said he wouldn't.

One day, however, he came to work smelling badly of alcohol. Our foreman called him to his office and said, "You are not allowed to drink, but you are half drunk. You'd better go home before you get hurt."

He went home under his own power, but not long thereafter he came to work and fainted on the job. We took him to the clinic emergency room. After the examination, the doctor said the young man had been drinking. The doctor told us that if he did not take good care of himself, the company could not take the risk of having him around. He might hurt himself, pass out, or die. In order to protect ourselves from serious consequences, we let him go with two weeks extra pay.

He left, and then he sued us. At that time, we didn't have a labor lawyer. Our corporate attorney recommended a young lawyer from his firm. After he reviewed the case, he came to our office to interview our foreman and plant manager. At the conference, he said, "We have a strong case. When we go to court, I—"

Before he could finish the sentence, I interrupted. "I don't want to go to court. I want to settle this out of court."

Confucius said: "We must try to stop the suits in court."

After a couple of months of negotiation, the lawyer settled the case by agreeing to pay the boy two thousand dollars. I personally delivered the check to him at his home. He walked down the stairs and signed the agreement releasing us from further responsibility. I handed him the check and said, "You'd better take good care of yourself, if you want to live long. You'd better quit drinking." He didn't say a word and went upstairs with the check.

Did we do the right thing by giving him money, even though we did not do anything unfair to him or against the law? What would happen to him eventually?

Going to court to settle a dispute is often the worst thing anybody can do; it wastes time and effort, and mostly benefits the lawyers. I feel it's usually preferable to find a way to settle things out of court. I would rather have given the money to this poor sick boy than have spent it on legal fees. Our new young lawyer wanted to go to court, hoping to make more money, rather than build a good relationship with us as a regular client. After this case, I never contacted him again.

Of course, the suit amounted to highway robbery. We were unfortunate to hire a person with diabetes who didn't take care of himself. A business is not a charity organization. It can make contributions to nonprofits to help the chronically ill, but hiring an employee like this boy really disrupted our operation. Such situations are out of the company's control.

After the diabetic case, I made a concerted effort to look for a competent labor lawyer to protect us from making legal mistakes in the future. I called a few friends to ask them for recommendations, but to my surprise I found that nobody had actually engaged a labor lawyer for his own company. I did not want to ask our attorneys, because they would only recommend specialists in their own firms. They did not really know many candidates to compare and select for me. Also, for an attorney to refer business to a member of his firm would promote his own prestige and gain him a small percentage of the billing received by the lawyer he recommended. I could have asked several attorneys at different firms for recommendations and chosen one among them by myself, but that would have offended the others.

Since this was not an urgent matter, I decided to wait and see what happened. Two months later, I received a flyer from the Manufacturers Association saying the next month's speaker would be Carol Manzoni, a labor lawyer. I went to the meeting and was so impressed that I introduced myself immediately after she finished her speech.

"Would you be interested in being our labor attorney?" I asked her.

She seemed pleased that someone would want to engage her then and there, and knew her speech had been a success. She asked me to call her at her office and gave me a business card. She probably thought, "Whoa, not so fast!"

When Carol Manzoni became our labor attorney, the first thing she did was to guide us to write our corporate manual, which systematically organized our company rules and regulations in a single book. Ever since then, we had never made a move with regard to employees without consulting her first. We always listen to what she tells us, and when we do not understand, she always explains in detail.

Once she told me, "John, if all my clients were like you, listening to me all the time, I'd go broke."

She spoke about a client of hers. The owner had serious trouble with an employee, and the employee sued him. The owner believed he was in the right, and legally he was. Carol suggested an out-of-court settlement that would cost him under one hundred thousand dollars, but he was a proud and stubborn man of German descent, and wanted to fight to the end. Eventually, it cost him over a quarter of a million dollars, a good part in legal fees. In conclusion, she said, "That's where I make my money," and laughed.

At Magenta, we have always tried to stay within the law. Labor law has been ever changing, however, and often it leaves loopholes for abuse. Some employees are greedy and lack honor. When they learn about the loopholes, they try to take advantage of the law or even attempt to cheat or blackmail employers.

Chinese proverb: "You may think, knowing the face, you know the person, but you do not know the heart."

One time, a smart-looking young lady came in to apply for an office job. She had worked for an old and large corporation for over seven years before the corporation went out of business. She had done all types of office work and seemed quite capable. She was married and had one young child.

We checked her references and talked to her previous employer, and they all said she was a good worker, so we hired her. She worked well for over a year and got pregnant. She told us right away, and we were happy for her.

But before we knew it, much to our surprise, we were in trouble. At first, she claimed she felt ill due to the pregnancy and took a day or two off. After a couple of weeks, she started to work on her own schedule. She came in on Monday, did not show on Tuesday, came in on Wednesday, and disappeared on Thursday. For the first two weeks, she took off two days each week and later took three days off a week.

This woman and her husband were both competent with computers. Months before, when I'd asked her about buying a computer, her husband had come to my office and shown me one. I casually remarked that since they both knew and enjoyed computers, they could go into some sort of computer business for themselves. I always like to encourage young people to start their own business, and I love to see them succeed. They had answered casually, saying they would think about it.

Now, by her staying away from work two or three days a week, I figured she and her husband were probably already planning or doing something on their own.

The law protects pregnant workers. Since pregnant women often become ill, they are permitted to take time off work, when they don't feel well. During and after childbirth, women can take more leave to recuperate and nurture the infant. Employers do not like to tango with pregnant women, but the law rightfully protects them.

In our case, however, the woman never was ill, but stayed home from work regularly to suit her schedule. She definitely took advantage of the law, because we could not prove that she wasn't sick. Nobody can say another person doesn't have a headache. For that matter, we couldn't even be sure she was really pregnant. She had no doctor's note.

I consulted Carol Manzoni, who said we couldn't do anything about it. So I called this employee to my office.

"We know you know that the law protects pregnant workers," I told her, "but you are taking advantage of the law and robbing us. I remember you mentioned that you and your husband were planning to start a family business. Why not do it honestly? I may be of some help to your venture. I don't like trouble, but if I have to, I will fight you. You know I can afford more than you can. Why not just resign quietly? I'll give you two months' pay to help you start your new business."

"I'll talk to my husband," she answered, without any shame.

"Tell him that to take the money and go is the best for you," I said. "I'll talk to my lawyer again. Come in tomorrow and see me."

The next day she informed me that she would quit, if we gave her five thousand dollars. I said her proposal was blackmail and out of the question. "You know I prefer to settle things peacefully," I explained, "but if you force me, I will do whatever I must. Somebody has already suggested I put a private detective on you. We may insist on putting you in jail. You think it over carefully and talk to me again tomorrow."

Here I bluffed. In truth, company business kept me so busy I didn't have time to fool around with a petty blackmailer. But I hoped my warning would give her something to worry about and might reduce the ransom.

After a week's negotiation, with Carol's approval, we settled the matter with the pregnant employee for four thousand dollars. When she came for the money, our receptionist let her in, and she walked directly to my office. Five people watched her disrespectfully, their eyes narrowed.

I took her to the office manager's desk to sign the resignation papers. She didn't look at anybody. Our manager gave her the check, and I looked her in the eyes.

"Aren't you ashamed?" I asked.

She didn't say a word and left with only a glance at me as she walked out the door.

Why would a smart person sell out her principles and dignity for so little? She would remember her blackmailing all her life and, I presume, would have no peace with herself, even if she could find some make-believe excuse for her deed. When she becomes old and gray, she can tell herself, "Oh, at that time, we needed the money so badly." Or she might say, "The company was not fair. They promoted Debbie instead of me. Anyway, I outsmarted the guy. They couldn't do a thing about it." But she'll always know in her heart that she extorted the money from people who had treated her well.

The reason I paid dear money to the blackmailer for peace and didn't fight for justice was that I had a business to run and no time to cure the ills of the human race or even the legal system. If we had really put a detective on her, and taken the case to court and won, the cost would have been much higher than the ransom money.

Until the loophole in the law is closed and employers can be protected from blackmail, we have to be very careful when we hire a female employee of child-bearing age, to make sure she is an honest person, even though I am sure we will not find one in a million who will blackmail us again, when she is pregnant.

A full-fledged mold maker requires a much longer and more demanding learning process than most other trades. To become an experienced mold repairman, a mold maker has to work at the mold shop of a plastic molding company for a long time. Because of this hardship in training, most young men shy away from the profession. A truck driver can make more money at the beginning without much training. Therefore, we've had difficulty finding qualified mold repairmen.

One day, an older man came into our office looking for a plastic mold maker's job. He was a mild-mannered man with a low voice and a smiling face. His hair was all white. The reason he had to ask for a position instead of being grabbed by a mold shop was that he was a die maker, not a plastic mold maker. Demand for die makers had been slowly decreasing, and he wanted to change professions for future job protection.

Our tool room foreman thought an experienced die maker could gradually learn to become a mold maker without much difficulty. In the meantime, he could also work on the simpler jobs in the tool room. We took him in at a slightly lower wage level than our other mold repairmen, and he was happy.

After a couple of years, this man began to show signs of discontent. Apparently, he thought that he had learned plastic mold repair and should make as much money as the more experienced mold makers. But he had not learned about solving molding problems, and we believed he was not worth as much as the other experienced men.

Then he complained about the high cost of health insurance for his family. Our company had always paid a large portion of the insurance premium for employees, but the family had to pay for themselves. Otherwise, it would be unfair to those who did not have a family, or whose families were already insured at other places. He didn't like our system.

We should have asked him to retire, but before we tried, he started to organize a union in the tool room. We were sure he knew that we didn't have enough people to have a union, and nearly all our mold makers were loyal employees who had many years of service with us. One of our mold makers told him face-to-face that he was crazy to talk about union in this shop.

But he knew the law. By trying to organize a union, he gained a suit of armor provided by the law. An employer cannot fire an employee because he tries to start a union, and proving that an employee was not fired for union activities would be difficult.

This man then began to work at a slow pace and make careless mistakes. We warned him, but didn't dare fire him or even ask him to retire. If we had, he surely would have sued us, claiming we tried to get rid of him because of his union activity.

After his unrealistic attempt at union organizing, we noticed he took less interest in his work, acted more timidly toward his coworkers, and his mind often was not on the job. Sure enough, an accident happened, and he got hurt. The insurance company took care of him for over a year, and then, he retired. Of course, the insurance company increased our premium later.

Once again our mistake was inadequate checking; before we hired him, we failed to learn that he had worked in a shop with a strong union

Another case involved a female employee. She was an African-American, over fifty years old, husky, and straightforward. She worked for us for nearly eight years, and I would say she was a useful worker.

All of a sudden, her behavior changed. First, she swore at a coworker for absolutely no cause and created a fight. After exchanging some bad words, she nearly punched the lady. The foreman stopped them in time. She then swore at the foreman.

The foreman reported the incident to the plant manager and then to me. Her behavior puzzled me. I thought she probably had had a bad day and was in a foul mood. But a couple of weeks later, she purposely refused to follow an instruction from the foreman. When the foreman asked her why she didn't do as she had been told, she swore at him again.

The foreman, the plant manager, and I had a meeting. The foreman suggested she wanted to be fired instead of quitting.

"I doubt it, because that does her no good," I said.

I called Carol Manzoni, who told us that we needn't be in a hurry to let the employee go as long as we had complete documentation of what she had done in our file. At the end of the meeting, we decided not to fire her until we found out just what she was up to.

Before long, the woman came to my office and asked to be transferred to the third shift. She said she wanted to take the auto mechanic training program offered by General Motors in the daytime. After completing the training program, she could get a much better job as an auto repairperson. I told her I wished her luck. We made the transfer right away, and she started working the third shift the following Monday.

But before the first week in the third shift was over, she had an argument with the third shift foreman, refusing to listen to him and swearing at him without any cause. When the foreman reported this incident, we reached the conclusion that she had been trying to get us to fire her for reasons we couldn't figure out. After conferring with our labor attorney, we fired her. She seemed quite unconcerned and quickly left.

We were confident she couldn't do anything to us, as we had compiled a complete file recording all her incidents or misbehavior. Within a month, we received a notice from the labor board indicating that she had sued us for racial and age discrimination.

We presented our documentation and sent our third shift foreman to appear in front of the judge. Our former employee did not show up in court that day. Our foreman, who was also an African-American, and who had worked for us for over fifteen years, answered all the judge's questions, and, of course, the answers favored the company. After the woman didn't show up for the second court date, the judge dismissed the case.

Based on our later conversations with other employees who had worked with her, we felt that some paralegal had told her she could get many thousands of dollars from the company for racial and age discrimination, if she got fired after working for the company for so many years. Later on, someone must have told her otherwise. Paralegals or even greedy lawyers often stir up troubles, persuading minority employees to sue their employers for the most remote reasons. What a shame!

Most of the cases of such abuses of the laws have occurred in the last few years, at least with our company. More people are suing now than even a few years ago. We can only hope that some day, this problem will be brought to the public's attention and the government will decide to close the legal loopholes. We need new laws that will protect employees and, at the same time, shield employers from being robbed or blackmailed by greedy opportunists.

Confucius said: "If you manage people by virtue and guide them with courtesy, they will know humility and follow the rules."

12

The Crisis

"Desperation promotes change; change opens new roads."

—Chinese proverb

Jim Adams inspected our plant the second year after we opened our doors, but we had to wait three years before his buyer at the IBM Corporation was willing to give us a try. Because we had done reliable work for them since that time, we became one of their most important suppliers of molded-plastic components.

Through the years, we had built a modern tool room for mold maintenance and repairs, then, set up a separate quality-control system specifically to meet IBM's requirements in addition to our standard system for other customers, including health-care companies.

Our diligence and our modern facilities combined to create a very close relationship with IBM. The majority of Mr. Adams's coworkers were from local farming families, decent, considerate folks without pretense. The relationship between our people and theirs deepened into trust and friendship. In three or four years they became our number-one customer in revenue.

In order to protect both the corporation and its suppliers, IBM Corporation established a rule stating that no more than thirty percent of a supplier's total annual revenue should come from the corporation.

This policy sounds simple, but abiding by it was very difficult. Here's why: Quite frequently, new models and new products replaced old ones. These product changes usually occurred within just a few years. While producing the current products, we had to take on projects in preparation for new models; otherwise, when the old product phased out, we would not be ready to replace it.

Magenta worked on innovations with IBM at all times. We took on whatever new projects they asked us to do; no one could be sure which project would be successful and which would fail. When a successful new project went into production, while the old product was still being sold, our business volume drastically increased, often exceeding thirty percent of our total revenue. This situation would be adjusted back to normal, when the old product was gradually eliminated.

The corporation had another rule dealing with new projects: If one was developed successfully within the budgeted expenditures and within the planned time schedule, the engineer in charge of the project would receive a promotion, if he hadn't had one in the near past. We saw two engineers advance, because they had worked on projects successfully with us. Obviously, this prompted more engineering teams to develop more projects with us, which presented further revenue-building opportunities.

Some projects were intended to develop a totally new product rather than update an existing one. If such an innovation became successful, then, we added a new income stream to our existing revenue.

With such a variety of situations, our business with this corporation often amounted to over thirty percent of our total revenue. But, because the buyers and engineers preferred working with us, the thirty percent rule was not strictly enforced, and no one worried about the possibility of future adversity.

Confucius said: "Man who has no long range concern will encounter problems close at hand."

While we did well with IBM Corporation, we lost business with health-care companies. For years, we had worked with a large health-care products company, but by the mid-1980s, its purchasing needs changed, because they built their own molding plant. To my knowledge, all large companies that had tried to mold their own plastic products had failed for various reasons, but this company did something smarter: They outsourced the difficult, troublesome, and short-run jobs, while their own plant molded only the long run and trouble-free products.

There was a catch: the outsource price could not be more than ten percent over the estimated price furnished by their molding department, which was always impracticably low. Insiders confided that their pricing did not include sales, administration, or even packaging costs. Thus, molders who bid and won their jobs did it by deliberately cutting their prices, when they desperately needed jobs to fill their machines. Soon, we were unable to get much production business from this company.

Magenta's work with this company was primarily in development or problem solving. If we successfully developed or solved a problem with a product, then Magenta won the business for production.

This arrangement also changed, however; even if we helped with development or improved a product, we could get the molding business for only one year and at a price not more than ten percent over the estimate made by their molding department.

This struck me as being very unfair. During the first year, the startup time might take several months, and the molder could not even make a full year of production. If we had helped them solve problems, we, naturally, would want to do the production for a few years at least, and at a fair price.

At first, we didn't know of this new rule. One project engineer came to see me with a diagnostic cup design and asked us to make samples. We did. Then he asked us to improve the samples we had made from their design. We spent a full year perfecting the design that had, by then, been completely redesigned by us. He and his company were happy and went into production. After one year, the project engineer came to see me again. He said, "John, since this cup is primarily being used in California, management wants to let the California people make it."

Before I could say anything, they took all the resins and the molds away, just like that.

I went to see the purchasing manager. He told me over lunch about the one-year rule. He emphasized, "The rule is not really new." In other words, they could apply the rule whenever it worked to their advantage. Where in this new policy was a sense of loyalty to suppliers?

This health-care company changed buyers every six months, to eliminate the possibility that buyers could build friendships with suppliers. They believed a cordial relationship would influence the buyer's judgment or even lead to corruption. The thinking behind this policy was the same as the one-year rule: Suppliers were the enemy. The company would not work hand-in-hand with the suppliers, so they could grow and prosper together.

Six months was not enough time for a new buyer to learn who offered quality products and quality services. Even if he studied the files on the suppliers, he could not appreciate the many intangibles present in a business relationship. Under such conditions, the suppliers had to compete on price alone. If we still wanted to offer superior products and service, our price would be not competitive. This policy certainly wasn't fair to the suppliers, and I doubt it was beneficial to their company in the long run.

We backed out silently.

Nevertheless, their project engineers and product managers still preferred to work with outsiders in developing or improving projects, because their own engineering department would never overtax themselves, and let somebody else in the company take credit for their success. The managers could ask an outside supplier to hurry, but would not dare pressure the engineering department of their own company.

One day, a friend of mine from this company came to my office and showed me a concept print for a packaging product.

"John," he said, "can you think about this concept and see if you like it? If you don't, come up with something better."

"My friend, I am sorry," I said without even looking at his concept. "I don't have as much spare time as I used to. Why don't you let your engineering people to do it? When you are ready for production, I'll be happy to bid on it."

He was quite surprised and very disappointed. Perhaps I should have explained to him we could not work under their current purchasing policies.

The health-care product manufacturers had been under tremendous pressure to reduce manufacturing costs from all sides: the government, the hospitals, the insurance companies, and the doctors. One company from which we had steady business tried to save money by moving their manufacturing facilities to Mexico, with headquarters in San Diego. We lost all our molding business with this company except for one product that was extremely troublesome. This matter made us very unhappy, but it was not a deathblow, as the volume we had with this company was not significant.

The respiratory-apparatus company, our first health-care products customer, continued to be a reliable customer for many years, until it was sold at about the same time as the other health-care company changed their purchasing policies. Then gradually, we lost their business, as the new management preferred to use their old suppliers.

With all the losses in business from the health-care industry, we had to plan how to replace the reduced revenue. Just at this difficult time, changes were made at the Kentucky plant of IBM.

Early in 1985, after we had been working for this corporation for nearly fifteen years, we put the finishing touches on a new, improved model of one of their popular products. They ordered two sets of production molds. Sometimes they preferred to put one set of molds at another molding shop, just to play it safe.

This time the engineer in charge told us they wanted us to ship one set of molds to their own plant in Kentucky.

"Somebody purchased some molding machines some time ago for a special project in their own plant," the engineer in charge explained, "but the machines were never used, because the project didn't go full steam. Now, they might want to utilize these machines." He ended by saying, "Anyway, that's the rumor I heard."

I figured they wanted to see if they could mold the products more cheaply themselves. So I talked to the buyer and offered to install more automation for the job and to reduce the price.

"I really don't know what to tell you," the buyer said. "The sales of the new model of this product are not as good as anticipated."

By December, we did not have many new jobs lined up, and our most important customer, the Kentucky plant, had not been ordering as much as usual for that time of the year. I told myself, "Don't worry; at year's end everybody is slow, because of the holidays. Business will pick up in January."

But by January, things became even slower. By February, orders were still not coming in as they should have.

In the first week of March, I went to Kentucky to see for myself what was going on. Over the years, Jim Adams had been promoted to superintendent in charge of manufacturing for the group we had been serving. The buyer took me to the superintendent's office, and the three of us sat down to talk.

Mr. Adams told me their company had been very happy to have enjoyed such a good relationship with us for so long. Then, he got down to business.

"The sales of the new model were not as good as we originally estimated," he said. "Two years ago, the company eliminated its sales force and let its distributors sell the products just at the time competition came in.

"When a potential buyer wanted to save money by giving up some good features of our product, the distributors recommended a simpler and cheaper Japanese model."

"I understand," I told him, but I felt as if a lead weight had settled in my gut.

"The poor performance of the new model and the gradual drop in sales of the old model created a bad situation for our company," he continued.

"Yes," I said.

"For years we have been all-out for automation," he went on. "Robots and other modern equipment have replaced many of our workers. In the past, our growth in new areas could always take up the displaced workers. This time, these people could not be retrained and put to work elsewhere. This condition has created an enormous problem for management. We never like to lay off employees."

Everybody in the office was quiet. They must have decided one or two years before to solve their labor problem by doing plastic molding themselves. They'd already bought the molding machines.

"We have workers and equipment," he said in a low voice. "I hate to take jobs away from our suppliers, but what can we do?"

At the end, he told me we would not get any new projects or jobs. They were considering letting our company produce components of the old model, which they had been doing themselves. After his long speech, he stood up and said, "Let me show you the plant."

First, he took me through the complete production line of the old model, just in case they needed to call upon us to do the job for them. Then he led me through rows of molding machines, many already installed and others still in crates.

"Wow! How many?" I could not help but cry out loud.

"Seventy-five," he answered.

They had bought seventy-five molding machines, large and small, from Germany a year before, and the project engineer had only told me they might want one set of molds from us for their plant. Hadn't he seen all of these monsters? The buyer had not told me anything, either, although he stopped sending me orders. Perhaps they had received instructions from top management to say nothing about this to the suppliers at that time.

Usually, when small but irritating things happen, I get upset; but when something serious occurs, I turn calm. This time, I was very calm. I was facing a financial catastrophe that would affect my business and all my employees. I would be partially shut down for quite a while, as our business with IBM had amounted to over thirty percent of our total revenue. What bad timing it was, just when the business with the health-care industry was dropping.

After we had lunch in the cafeteria, I went with the buyer to his office. A couple of friends came in to say hello. Magenta had a good reputation and relationship there, but that meant nothing if they pulled their molds from us.

Chinese proverb: "Next to a large tree, it is easy to establish roots."

My company had grown as I created an excellent relationship with a large corporation.

But another Chinese proverb says, "Serving a king is like serving a tiger; it can kill you any time."

This means that just like a tiger, a king can kill you any time he feels like it, for any reason. At the time, we were with IBM, IBM was the king; now they were killing us with a policy change without warning. I was nearly ruined, when IBM stopped needing us. For me, "serving (only) a king" turned out to be a big mistake, one we would never make again.

Confucius said: "When you make a mistake, don't hesitate to correct it."

Our health-care customers had not only turned ruthless toward their suppliers, but were also uncooperative with their own out-of-town plants. Those plants would rather buy from outside suppliers, if the price were low enough not to arouse complaints from their molding department.

The moment I got back to my office, I telephoned the buyers of two of the out-of-town plants of this health-care company. One buyer had begun to get angry with his own molding department.

I made appointments and visited them right away. They were happy to see an outside molding person visit them. I told them squarely, "One of our largest customers has just decided to do in-plant molding, and we have to replace the business we're going to lose. I can offer you low prices on your current needs with our normal good service."

In about three months, I received several molds from these people

Magenta had not employed a full-time salesperson during the years. With one, perhaps we could have grown faster and might not have had to depend on one large customer to survive. At the time, though, I did not think we could make good use of a sales staff for custom molding. I never realized that I could have an extra salesperson in addition to myself. Now, these thoughts were too late to help.

I sat in my office, quietly searching for the best way to meet this crisis. A crisis is something we have to get through. I said to myself, "We must find a way to save the situation. This is an opportunity for us to come up with something good and to correct our past mistakes."

In a few moments, I concluded that the best way to solve the problem was to buy a small company that had proprietary products. Right! That's it!

Of course, I had to add a sales force first. I picked up the phone and called a friend of mine, a molding-equipment representative who had been around the industry for many years. I explained the situation, then said, "You know so many people. Can you recommend someone?"

"I'll send you names and phone numbers," he answered. "You can talk to them."

"I also want to buy a small company with proprietary plastic products," I continued. "Do you know some business brokers?"

"That I can't help you with," he responded. Then, "Wait! I know a guy who used to work for a large health-care product company. I heard that he quit and became a business broker. I'll get you his name and phone number."

Within a few days, I had called all the sales representatives my friend had recommended, but they were all firmly tied up with other plastic molders. None wanted to start a new relationship with Magenta. Normally, to cultivate a good sales representative takes years, just like cultivating a good customer. I couldn't blame them for not wanting to try me out.

I placed advertisements in newspapers and professional magazines for sales representatives and received several responses. I interviewed a few and came to terms with two of them. But in a short time, I found out they were not right for the work we needed. I couldn't find a single one with whom we could make long-range plans.

At that moment, the road through sales representatives came to a dead end.

I contacted the business broker my friend had told me about. He came to my office, and we got acquainted. He gave me several leads. The first one was in Wisconsin-a very small company whose products were dying out. The others were of no value at all.

I called several business brokers I found in the yellow pages, and they provided more leads. One was a shoe-sole manufacturer in Texas. I went there and found an old plant with old equipment in a business I knew nothing about. Even if it had offered a worthwhile line of products, I would have had to invest in all new equipment to do a good job. I didn't bother to learn more. The owner, an old man, and I had a quick lunch together, and somehow I paid the bill.

When I returned to Chicago, a friend of mine told me about a molding company in California that made plastic boxes for electronic products. I flew to California and learned their production plant was in Idaho.

The boxes had no patent protection and were just commodity items, but the company seemed to have done a pretty good business. Somewhat interested, I went to Idaho to look at the plant. Although the situation wasn't ideal, I thought it might save our neck. Then, they insisted on selling the plant with the business, because they owned the building. What would I do with an industrial plant in Idaho?

Back in Chicago, I visited two local plants and traveled to see another in Ohio, but came away disappointed. None could help us. These plant visits took more than three months, and at the end of all the traveling, I felt depressed and mentally worn out.

Suddenly, an old Chinese story flared up in my mind: A farmer lived in the northern region bordering the rebellious tribes who often invaded the villages and robbed the people. One day, his mare ran away. He was very sad, because that was the only horse he had.

After only a few days, the mare came back, and with her came two beautiful stallions. He then felt very happy. He knew how to ride a horse, but the stallions were wild. When he tried to mount one of them, he was thrown off and broke a leg.

He told his wife, "After all, the whole thing is a bad omen."

Before long, the northern tribes invaded China again. The government needed more soldiers and started to draft young men who lived in the border region to protect their farmland. The farmer was not drafted because of his broken leg. Later, he learned that many of his neighbors had been killed in battle, but his life had been spared.

"After all, we had good luck that our mare ran away," he told his wife.

Referring to this story, the Chinese proverb says, "The border farmer lost his horse, but how do you know it will not bring good luck?"

This story made me feel we still had hope. We had lost IBM Corporation, but how did we know it wouldn't turn out to be a good luck? I regained my energy and started again to try to solve the problem.

First, what was I going to do with all my extra workers? Management had to stay, no matter what; they would be difficult to replace, when we regained our business. I also had to keep my special skilled workers. Training new ones would take time and money. All these employees were relatively well paid.

In order to reduce expenses, the only people we could consider laying off temporarily were machine operators and floor boys. Many of them were newly hired and easily replaced. Because they were lower-paid employees, laying them off did not give me much financial relief. We, eventually, laid off about ten percent of the lower-paid working force.

What else could we do to survive? I wondered. Experienced people say that things never get as bad as we fear or as good as we expect. If this were to hold true for us, our outcome would be somewhere between bankruptcy and sudden growth.

13

A Friend Saves the Day

"Heaven lays no dead-end road."

—Chinese proverb

"Hey, this is Al! Long time no see," the caller said. "How are you?"

Al had been in my car pool, when I worked for the research and development group.

"Fine," I said. "How are you enjoying retirement?"

"Oh, it's great just loafing around," he said. "Hey, I heard the closure division is trying to sell their plastic-closure business. Those metal closure people don't know plastics. You interested?"

This was the metal closure division of the can company I had worked for so many years ago.

My pulse rate went up, and I answered, "Oh, man, am I interested!" I told him I had been looking for months to acquire a small company or proprietary products.

He gave me the name of the person to contact. It occurred to me that since I'd worked in the research and development group of this can company, I could be considered an alumnus. Maybe they would take it easy on me when we worked on a deal.

Chinese proverb: "A long night creates more dreams."

I called the man immediately. I firmly believe in this proverb! The faster I proceeded, the less chance there was for obstacles to materialize. All my traveling during the past several months had resulted in disappointments. This was a really good opportunity. I had to make it work.

135

The next week, I met the boss, his assistant, and his manager of plastic closures. The headman was a bureaucratic type, a typical corporate man, and his assistant showed little interest in the matter. The manager, a clean-cut young fellow, had the detailed information on the plastic closures.

He told me that over ten years before, the company had bought a child-resistant closure company, but they had not done much with it. First, their core business dealt with metal closures. Second, the plastic-closure business was small and had shown practically no growth, so management wanted to dispose of it.

I told them my business history, and they seemed happy to learn I had been a company member. We knew some of the same people. We scheduled another meeting, at which they would show me the detailed figures of the whole closure business. This would include the list of closures, sales, list of customers, inventory, special equipment, and so forth.

Upon returning to my office, I called our accountant Bernie and Byron, our banker, and told them what was going on. They knew what had happened with IBM Corporation and were quite excited for me, probably, in part, because I was so excited myself. They both wished me good luck. Neither one even asked me how much the deal might cost.

At the second meeting, the boss came in to say hello, then left. The assistant did not show at all. The manager gave me the lists of closures, customers, sales for each closure, assembling machines, molds, patents, and inventories.

"Study these lists and figures," he said, "then give us a price for the whole business."

After looking over the information with Bernie, we came up with a figure. We knew the plastic-closure business had never been important to them. In ten years, their research-and-development people had not come up with any new plastic-packaging products. Since nobody in top management had paid much attention to the plastic-closure business, we figured they would sell it at any price, as long as it made the responsible people look fairly good in the accounting book and smart to the top management.

First, I went to see their molding and assembling plant. The manager, a young man, took me to his office and gave me a brief picture of what they had and what they were doing. He showed me the plant. Several molding machines were fairly new and reasonably maintained, but not as clean as ours. These machines were not for sale, and I was glad I didn't have to take them. There were six assembling equipment, and only two were running. Each jammed up a couple of times, when the manager and I were there. These six machines did not amount too much. Nobody was in the quality-control room, and I saw no modern instruments.

When we got back to the manager's office, he started to talk. He told me he only molded some closures in his plant. Most of the closure molds were in custom molding shops. He said he would draw up a list of molds and where they were, and he offered to take me to those shops to see how they ran.

Before I left, he said, "I've been in this molding business for over ten years, and we have improved the molding cycles tremendously in the last couple of years. The trouble is I can't get enough good help, although the girl in the quality-control room is excellent."

But in examining the molded closures in the assembling area, I could see he had quality problems both inside and outside his plant.

The next day, he and I visited a molding shop where he had placed three molds of one type of closure. One mold was running. The foreman at the shop showed us his plant. I took them to lunch, and we had a nice conversation. The manager suggested we should visit another molding company I knew something about. I told him we didn't have to visit that company.

Actually, I had a reason for not wanting to go to that company: I wanted to avoid seeing a man who had formed a bad impression of me after an incident with a man called The Operator. I'd met The Operator while working in the can company's research and development group. After several internal reorganizations that resulted in many people being laid off or transferred, he kept his job through office politicking and machinations. The last time, I had talked to him, a few years before, he was with the bottle division of the can company. He'd called and asked for a quote on a plastic cap for bottles, claiming that the present molder could not make good caps.

After I quoted a price, The Operator quickly moved the mold from a large molding company to our plant. Our tool room checked out the mold and found it in poor shape and in need of costly repair. When I gave The Operator the news, he insisted we try to run it. After we molded some defective caps, I asked him to return the mold to the original molder, who had experience with the mold and could fix it at lower cost than we could and produce good caps for him.

He took the mold back to the original molder. I could not imagine what he might have said about us in regard to this matter, but he said to me, "I was only trying to help. You know, I am available", hinting that he wanted a job with us.

I did not respond to his remark, but thought to myself, "In those many years when we worked at the same company, I never wanted to have anything to do with you. I should have kept my distance from you now."

Due to this incident, the owner of the original molding company probably thought I'd tried to steal his business. I'm sure he formed a bad impression of me, because a couple of years after this, a mutual friend suggested I go see the man's plant layout. When I telephoned him, he turned me down.

This was the same molding plant the can company manager wanted me to visit. Naturally, I did not want to meet the man who had formed such a strong misunderstanding toward me. Even had I tried to explain the situation, I wasn't sure whether he would listen to me or to The Operator.

Chinese proverb: "Ill will should be resolved rather than provoked."

I arranged a third meeting with the manager of the closure division and arrived early. We were sitting in the conference room when the boss came in. He shook my hand and said, "John, as you may not know, another man is looking at the situation."

I didn't believe him; I figured he was trying to get a better offer from me. He could have said, "John, you'd better not cut the price too low. If you do, we'll look for other buyers." Even such talk would have amounted to no more than bluffing. I believed they actually didn't want to publicize the sale of the business, because they didn't like people in the can industry to know about this matter. They probably preferred to dispose of the plastic-closure division quietly, if not secretly.

I offered them the price I'd originally decided on with my accountant, not influenced by the remark made by the closure division boss. The price was fair to both parties. They didn't quibble, and we completed the deal quickly.

I believe the deal saved our company. My accountant was happy because he could write off tools, equipment, and patents to save taxes. My banker friend believed the deal must be good, because he always trusted whatever I did. Byron had said, "If it is all right with John, it is all right with me." I was so lucky that my banker friend trusted me this much..

Once we closed the deal and paid the money, the transition period consisted of straightening out some confusion. We spent three months adjusting the inventory records to agree with the actual counts, shipping all the raw materials and finished goods to our location, and disposing of the rejects. Pulling all the molds into our plant to be repaired took nearly six months. The assembling machines also badly needed repair, and some of them had to be practically rebuilt to a better design.

During this time, I had lunch with the former manager of the plastic-closure business of the can company. He told me that they had forgotten to mention the existence of some plastic-closure experimental tools at the Research and Development department of the closure group. Since we knew those people had done nothing of value to the plastic closures, we just ignored that matter.

Although we missed seeing what their Research and Development department had done with new plastic closure development, we did inherit a safety closure lawsuit. After drinking a few cans of beer, a man had sprayed lighter fluid from a can with our plastic closure onto the burning charcoal of a grill. A flame had shot up and burned his face. He sued the can manufacturer, the plastic-closure manufacturer, the lighter-fluid packager, the lighter-fluid dealer, and the store. Eventually, he won sixty thousand dollars, and his lawyers collected seventy thousand dollars. Of course, the insurance companies paid all these costs.

Before we bought the plastic closure business, we had been shy about safety closures and child-resistant closures, because we didn't want to get involved in lawsuits of this kind; but since we were now deeply into the safety closure business, we had to overcome our concerns about such consequences.

In the meantime, we began checking the credit of the closure dealers before we made shipments, and we started to make routine collections. We didn't have many collection problems with custom molding customers; they were mostly larger companies, and their production molds were at our plant. They paid us regularly, as they needed productions periodically. With closure dealers we had to be more careful, because some dealers did not like to pay bills.

After about six months, we felt settled and comfortable as owners of the new enterprise. During this organizing period, the closure business had been going on as usual. Our loss of revenue caused by the pullout of the Kentucky IBM plant had been replaced almost overnight by the closure business.

During the startup period, I visited all the large closure customers, who were mostly on the East Coast. I assured them we would do our best to serve them. I also told them we were top plastic molders, as evidenced by the fact that we had been qualified suppliers for IBM Corporation as well as health-care companies.

At the end of this round of visits, on the airplane coming home, my mind wandered. The people in the East seemed happy with us as their supplier. They might have thought we were a small company and thus easier to deal with, but I found them less open and frank than Midwesterners. I was confident we could work with them in a cooperative spirit, drawing on my few years as a resident of New York City.

To my pleasant surprise, the people at the large health-care corporation in New Jersey we had gained with the closure business proved just as nice as the people from Kentucky. I began to believe that the culture of the company rather than the location determined the behavior of the people, and that the culture of a company, organization, or even a country can be acutely sensed or felt by an outsider.

Now, I looked out the airplane window and saw bright sunshine over a sea of white clouds. Imagine, if my friend had not told me about this closure business, or if he had told somebody else instead of me, what would have happened to us? I reconfirmed my philosophy: "Always be nice to everybody, no matter who he or she might be. You never know."

Confucius said: "A gentleman should always be modest and compatible with others."

The moment I arrived at home I called my friend Al and invited him and his wife to dinner. At Christmas time, I sent him an expensive gift to show my appreciation. He called and told me he had not expected to receive such a wonderful present. Regardless, he was happy that the closure business had worked out for me.

Confucius said: "Gentleman wants to be slow to speak but quick to act."

The day after I came back from the East, I called several friends to tell them we had just bought a plastic closure business from the can company and would need a man to run the closure division. "Please see if you can think of anyone," I requested. "If not, please spread the word for me."

For a long time, I received no response. One day, the *Packaging* magazine sales representative stopped by to say hello. I asked him to recommend a man to run our new closure division. "I told several friends and also registered with a couple of executive search firms," I said, "but so far no luck. Can you think of somebody?"

"I'll see what I can do," he said.

The day after, he called me and said, "I've thought of someone. You know the plastic-cap company in Chicago? The general manager has just retired. He may be able to help."

"This company never did any manufacturing, right?" I asked.

"That is correct," he said.

"Then he must have started as a salesman," I guessed.

"That I don't know," he responded. He gave me the man's name and phone number.

I called James Jackson right away and explained my needs. He said he would like to know more about our business, and we made an appointment for him to come see our plant.

During our first meeting, I noticed that Mr. Jackson was an old-fashioned gentleman, very well mannered, and wearing a sharply pressed suit with a color-matching tie. Having been the general manager of a plastic-closure sales company, I thought he should be able to help us sell our specialty closures. He seemed quite excited about the opportunity.

After his visit, I asked a few people about him. Those who knew him all said he was decent and honest. At first, I thought I would hire him as a salesman. If he worked out, then he could become the boss of the division. But when I offered that suggestion, Mr. Jackson didn't like it. He had been the general manager at his previous job and saw my offer as a demotion. I had a contract drafted with him as the manager of our closure division.

When Mr. Jackson joined us, the first thing he did was work with the advertising agency to make brochures for all the patented closures. He knew a lot of people in the closure-related industries. Some of his friends and acquaintances wanted to be our representative or dealer for our closures, but none really had the qualifications.

One thing I particularly noticed was the fact that Mr. Jackson paid a lot of attention to his office, the furniture, the hanging of paintings, and who would be his secretary, but said little about his plans to make the division grow. I assigned a young woman to do his correspondence, but he didn't need a full-time secretary. Even I, as president, did not have my own secretary.

Chinese proverb: "Picked up the sesame seeds but missed the watermelons."

Next, I turned my energies toward new product development. Although the closures we had bought from the can company had customers, I believed the closures were too complicated in design and too difficult to produce perfectly. We had to make good use of the breather period to develop closures of our own.

A friend of mine suggested I talk to a plastic closure and packaging engineer working with a successful plastic closure company. I called and told him we'd just got into the plastic closure business and needed all kinds of help. He told me he had retired from the closure company and would be interested in seeing what we had. I invited him to visit with us.

Mr. Swanson was a big fellow who'd come from Europe years before. He told me he had traveled worldwide and attended many plastic product and packaging shows. Although I could not judge his creativity, he obviously knew a lot about closures. After we met and talked a couple of times, I engaged him as our closure division's technical and marketing consultant. I asked him to participate in our weekly new-product meetings, and he did.

After several months, because nothing came out of these meetings, we stopped them, and our closure consultant came in only when needed. I have always believed that creation cannot be done at meetings. Inventing is an artistic process and should be worked on by individuals in their own time and place.

Our new closure division manager liked staying in the office and not traveling. That might have been due to his age. I started to look for a younger salesman. Our closure consultant recommended a salesman who worked at the closure company he used to be with. He said he knew this man had a very good track record. His biggest account was a famous household product company in Ohio.

I made an appointment with the salesman for an interview. Mr. Hayes was soft spoken and walked slowly, but his record indicated that he had sold a great many closures. I thought to myself, "He must have some special skill to have sold all those closures."

Our division manager thought Mr. Hayes was a nice fellow, and we hired him. Within a few months, we reached the conclusion that this young salesman didn't like to travel either, in spite of his promise to knock on doors. He talked to potential customers mostly by phone, although he visited local companies. I began to wonder how these two men could have such good track records, when they did not like to call on people. I decided to wait and see.

Mr. Jackson agreed with me on the importance of new product development. He made contact with a large salt company, among others. The company wanted a handy spout for a large container of the salt used to melt ice. We started to develop such a package. In six months, we came up with a side-pour closure. Mr. Jackson showed the model to the packaging boss of the salt company, who told him their company had planned to get out of the ice-melt business and had no more need for a closure with a large pouring spout.

This came as a big disappointment to us, but we believed the need for an ice-melt dispensing package was real, so we went ahead to develop it on our own. Meanwhile, we contacted many ice-melt companies, including Canadian firms, asking them if a side-pour dispensing closure for ice melt was needed, and if they would prefer it to the standard dispenser. All answers came back positive.

We also surveyed various powder-product companies and other potential users of pouring and spreading packages. The results were also mostly favorable, so we decided to go ahead and make a production mold. Although it involved quite a large investment and thus a big risk, we felt the outlay was justified because the potential was very promising.

We organized our closure division on a limited scale. Everyone was poised to make progress, and we did. This side-pour closure later received a golden award from *Packaging* magazine.

By the time we got our closure division in place, we needed the employees we had laid off during the crisis. Our office manager, Geri, called to ask them to return to work. According to the rule we had to call the people in descending order of seniority three times in the evening. If there was no answer, we could continue down the list. If we preferred not to have someone come back, Geri called the person early in the evening, hoping they were not home.

To our disappointment, the good workers had already found jobs and could not or did not want to return to a company that had laid them off. Geri told me we'd lost two upcoming young men and four reliable machine operators. All those who returned were borderline workers. After this experience, I became convinced that the best way to survive a crisis is to find more business quickly instead of laying off employees. The more business we could gain, the fewer employees we would have to lay off.

14

The President

"When people have the same will, dirt turns into gold."

—Chinese proverb

In the early 1980s, I began to think about retirement and finding someone to replace me for the future. I had the idea of finding an up-and-coming young engineer who could work with us for a few years, then take charge of the whole operation, if he proved capable.

A certain young man came to mind, from the Kentucky plant. I had worked with him and thought he was capable. I asked him if he would work for Magenta, but did not tell him what I had in mind. He turned me down, saying, "In addition to working at the corporation, I also have a side business working on my farm. I cannot leave Kentucky."

A couple of years later, I realized we were lucky he had not joined us. Otherwise, we both would have been disappointed, because I would not have made him our president.

Years later, Jim Adams told me that IBM had learned about my trying to hire this engineer. I did not show any emotion, but actually, felt very much disturbed. The young fellow should never have told anyone about it. Had he wanted to come, I would have asked for approval from the management of the corporation. When he refused, I had no cause to discuss my intention with the management. Now, that he told them about my offer, the management would think I had tried to steal their employee. In the future, I resolved to be very careful, if I ever tried to hire someone away from one of my customers; most people cannot keep secrets.

Chinese proverb: "There is no wall that wind cannot pass over."

A few years after this incident, I began to think about partial retirement. I became more serious about finding the right man. I put advertisements in professional magazines and received some responses. After sorting and interviewing, I hired an engineer, a sincere person from Pennsylvania, as manager in charge of engineering for our company. After a few months, I reached the conclusion that he was not sharp enough to take high-level responsibilities. I helped him find another job and loaned him money for relocating his family. I felt guilty, though, for moving him from Pennsylvania to Chicago, then sending him elsewhere.

After carefully thinking it over, I realized I had made the mistake, because I didn't know what kind of person I wanted. I'd always had the notion I should hire someone below the position of president, and the man should possess the qualities needed to become president later, after gaining experience with us. So far, this approach had not worked, perhaps because predicting the development of a person's potential is difficult. "Building" a president this way would be truly a formidable task.

Large corporations often hire chief executives from outside, although they have many executives within the company from which to choose.

Shortly thereafter, our Kentucky plant crisis arose. Following that, came the startup of the closure division. By then, our need for a president or a person who could be promoted to president became more urgent.

Our closure division manager continued to create doubt in my mind about his ability to manage and grow. Although Mr. Jackson had a good reputation and past record, I had found in him a lack of drive, shortness of stamina, and little vision. He paid attention to such petty things as printing the company name on the plastic silos or getting a post-office mailbox in front of our company building.

The salesman who had a good past record also somehow lacked a sense of urgency. Mr. Swanson sat in his office most of the time, talking on the telephone more than going out selling face-to-face. I firmly believe that people do not want to buy anything from someone with whom they are not acquainted, unless what they want is a standard commodity item. Because of this weakness, we needed a person to take over leadership responsibilities quickly.

I decided to look for a president outright. I carefully defined the position and the characteristics of the person I wanted to fill that position. I contacted several executive headhunters and spread the word among friends. A few weeks passed, and I received no responses from the agencies at all. I placed advertisements in professional magazines and newspapers, but these did not draw the right type of people. The wording in the advertisements must not have correctly and clearly defined the position.

Frustrated, I engaged a personnel consultant recommended by one of our attorneys. He was supposed to write and place the advertisements for us. Then, he was to screen the applicants and interview those he thought had possibilities. From among the people he interviewed, he would recommend the most qualified to me for interview.

Later, I found out that he, actually, had not interviewed any applicants himself. Instead, he just sent all the resumes to me for review and flagged some of the applications for interview. From the resumes, I selected and interviewed four or five people. Then I received recommendations from agencies and friends. Altogether I read close to two hundred resumes and interviewed a dozen people, but found none suitable for the position.

The consultant gave me a book titled *The Evaluation Interview*. With it he sent a false invoice for his expenses. I called him about it, and he corrected it without quibbling or apology. We paid him off and said goodbye.

One of my closure dealers recommended a man who, at the time, worked as president of a plastic-bottle company. I had several telephone conversations with him, and he sounded interesting. I intended to invite him to come for an interview, but sent him our organization chart first to show him the scope of our operation. In a few days, he sent the chart back to me with a note saying he thought we were very well organized and made one small change to the chart: He added a block under the president and filled it in with the word: secretary. Apparently, he believed a president should have a personal secretary.

From this small indication, I could see he was not my type. I never had a personal secretary, and never felt I needed one just to show my importance. How important you are depends on how much you accomplish. Since Geri had been promoted to office manager, she did typing for me besides her other duties. We did not have much correspondence with outside people and very few memos inside our company.

A memory came to mind: Almost ten years before, I had visited a large and well-automated plastic-closure manufacturing plant owned by an out-of-town company. The offices were lined up around a spacious rectangular indoor courtyard. Secretarial desks were placed in front of most of the offices, and five or six of the desks were occupied by secretaries. I didn't know their duties, but noticed one secretary filing her fingernails. A few years later, this manufacturing plant was sold. With this recollection in mind, I did not proceed with the interview with the bottle-company president.

A few more months passed, and I'd practically exhausted all my leads, so I started over, reminding my friends to be on the lookout for a president for me. After a couple of months, our former closure consultant called me.

"John, I've got somebody just right for you. The timing is perfect."

"Who? Who is the man?" I asked with great interest.

"The vice president in charge of manufacturing at the plastic-closure company where I used to work," he said. "His name is Michael Illenberger. He just started looking for a position in this area, because the company has decided to move the manufacturing facilities to Wisconsin, and he doesn't want to leave, because his wife is teaching here."

I made an appointment with this man right away. We met several times for lunch and had leisurely conversations. We seemed to agree in a variety of areas concerning management principles, attitudes, and style, although we had grown up quite differently. He had risen within corporation organizations, while I had been an entrepreneur throughout.

A corporate man gets to the top by stepping up the ladder. On the way, he has to pass many competitors. To do that, he has to work hard and be careful not to make big mistakes. As a result, the corporate man tends to be competitive, conservative, and more watchful about capital layout and expenditures than the entrepreneur.

Selling a new product to a large corporation is one of the most difficult tasks for a salesman to tackle. The main reason is that the decision-makers are corporate men. Will the customer take a chance on making a change in the way things have always been done? Will he risk the money? If the change is successful, he takes the credit with many other people involved in the project. If the change fails, he loses his job.

The vice-president in charge of manufacturing was engineering-trained and had a head for details. These generalized characteristics of a corporate type would certainly make him the man to maintain our company status. If I was right about his being capable, he probably could make our company grow. He seemed in harmony with our company culture, open door, fair to all, no pretense or showy tendencies. Sure, an entrepreneur tends to explore, develop new ideas, and take risks, but I had the feeling that in time, working in our entrepreneurial environment, he could evolve into an entrepreneurial-type leader.

The company Mr. Illenberger had grown up with was not a large, global corporation. I guessed he would eventually find his professional life more exciting, more fun, and more rewarding at the helm of a small company. All in all, I became confident he would be the man who could run Magenta without me.

Sunzi wrote: "A general should possess five characteristics: wisdom, kindness, trustworthiness, bravery, and discipline."

I would say a company president should be: intelligent, understanding, honest, courageous, and a leader.

Without working together for a long time, it would be difficult to judge whether a person meets these criteria. But as far as I could see, the man I had in mind to be our president did not show any negative signs in these categories.

I decided to bring Mr. Illenberger in as president. In addition to his salary, bonus, profit sharing, and insurance, I offered him a free hand in running the company operations. I would follow my usual principle: If I don't trust the person, I won't give him the responsibility; if I trust the person, I will let him do his thing.

Chinese proverb: "If you doubt a person, don't use him; if you use a person, don't doubt him."

Some entrepreneurs hate to entrust responsibility to others and always want to control everything themselves. I preferred to imply, if not say outright, "I trust you. Go ahead and perform. I eagerly await your accomplishments." The person will then have self-confidence, take risks, and create.

I told Mr. Illenberger he only needed to ask me for advice under two conditions: When he himself could not make up his mind and wanted my opinion, and when a large sum of money was involved.

Chinese proverb: "When huge rewards are offered, brave people will come forward."

I always believed in this saying, so I also offered our new president a two-percent bonus on company profit before taxes. Such an incentive would be a powerful motivation to anybody. Without handsome incentives, why should a president work extraordinarily hard? After all, this was not his own company.

After Michael Illenberger came to our plant, saw our facilities and workers, and met our managers, he agreed to join us and signed the employment contract. Once he came on board, a thought came to my mind: What would be the attitude of our new president toward our factory workers? Usually, a corporate man does not have the opportunity to work with factory employees, whereas an entrepreneur has labored with the employees from the beginning. Thus the corporate man tends to have less feeling or respect for the factory workers.

To his credit, Michael knew how to manage by rules, regulations, and procedures better than a born entrepreneur. I thought this might be good for our company, because we had become bigger, had more people, and should be run by standardized policies rather than by personal relationship.

I would have to wait and see how our president would behave in this regard. Each true leader has a different personality and manages business differently, but despite the diversity, they all work.

I was reminded of a historical story: During the later part of the Qing dynasty in China, the government was badly managed. A strong rebellious group threatened the dynasty, but the army had no morale and could not fight.

The emperor chose an honorable scholar with a strong personality to build a new army to fight the rebellion. Although the lieutenants and soldiers were not professional fighters, they eventually won the war, because they were totally loyal to the leader. They passionately followed his orders, because he had such a kind heart. Historians put it this way: "His men did not have the heart to be disloyal to him, and his new army became a strong army."

He, indeed, was an entrepreneur. Years later, the leadership of this army was passed on to a professional general coming up through the ranks. He was such a strong disciplinarian that nobody dared disobey him. He depended on rules and regulations, not on loyalty, to control the army. I would classify him as a corporate man.

When this general retired, a civil-service official took over the leadership of the army. This intellectual set up laws that were simple and clear. The soldiers could not find ways to disobey him. He also had a useful army until the dynasty collapsed. Both the general and the civil official did a good job of managing the army, although they did not have compassion for their men, and their men had little loyalty toward them.

In the modern business world, a corporate man probably is more effective than an entrepreneur to run a complicated operation. The corporate man would be more successful and have more fun, however, if he possessed an entrepreneurial attitude and spirit.

In 1990, when our new president reported to work, the operation was running normally. As Michael became familiar with the people and the environment, I went to his office to talk some business.

"Everyone in every department is in place, and everything is functioning," I told him. "Many elements need improvements, though. For instance, our qual-ity-control area needs help, and our tool room needs to be expanded."

"If I want to make any personnel change, I'll let you know first," he said.

"Fine," I answered. "But what I really want to discuss with you today is our closure division manager. He is not doing the job and isn't capable of building up the organization."

Our president said, "I understand he used to be the general manager of the famous closure sales company."

"Yes, he was," I explained. "But I just found out that he started there as office manager and not as a salesperson, as I'd thought. He was primarily an order taker. He claimed he was the one who sold the push-and-pull cap, but I'm not sure."

We decided to wait for a while. When Michael formulated his opinion, we would talk again.

After a couple of months, both Michael and I reached the conclusion that the closure division manager should go.

"We have to persuade him to retire," I said. "You have seen the employment contract with him. Mike, you are a better negotiator than I am. You can get a better deal than I can. See what you can do."

"I'll try to work out some retirement arrangement," he said.

In a few months, our president made a deal for the manager to retire. Then Michael began taking charge of the closure business and hired another salesman. He merged the closure business with other company functions.

As for Mr. Swanson, he had been with us for a couple of years, but still mostly stayed in the office, talking on the phone. He did obtain a project from a local company that turned out to be successful, and we gave him credit for this busi-ness, although our engineering and development people should have taken credit, also.

One day, I passed by Mr. Swanson's office. Since he did not look busy, I lei-surely walked in and casually asked, "How does the food company in the East like our liquid spout?"

"They are interested in it and told us not to show it to anybody else," he replied. After a few moments, he added, "They are waiting for our revised model."

"Are our people working at it?" I asked.

"I don't know," he said, "but the buyer told me they were not in a hurry."

This disturbed me, but I managed to smile and say, "Of course, they are not in a hurry. But we are! We have to be in a hurry, because we are the people who are trying to market a product. If we don't treat it as urgent business, we most likely will not make it. For that matter, any person who doesn't do things in an urgent manner cannot go far."

He listened and agreed.

Another of my lifelong principles has been this: If it is all right to do something either today or tomorrow, I do it today, because the unexpected can happen. Then, I have an extra day to adjust as necessary. I thought of telling Mr. Swanson about my principle, but did not. I figured he would listen and agree, but never be able to practice it.

Months later, the time came for Mr. Swanson to replace his old car. Our president told him that, from now on, all sales personnel would drive a Taurus.

"I have a Maxima. Can't I still have one?" he asked.

Our president said that wouldn't be fair to others. When Mr. Swanson had first come to Magenta, he had been the only salesman. He had told me he liked to drive a Maxima, and I said okay, not having paid attention to the name of the car. I didn't know the Maxima was not only more expensive, but also a Japanese car. Magenta and I buy American products whenever possible.

By this time, Mr. Swanson probably knew we didn't appreciate salespeople staying in the office most the time. Eventually, he found a job close to his home and quit.

Thinking the whole thing over, I saw I had actually been at fault. I told my people not to hire anyone who walked slowly, but I had hired Mr. Swanson on his past record and ignored his slow walk. I told this to our president. Michael smiled and said he knew of an owner of another small business who didn't hire people who walked slowly.

I was surprised to know another person existed who had such a notion. People say there are two types of salespersons. One is the hunter type. They get out to hunt. The other is the farmer type. They stay home and wait to harvest. Mr. Swanson certainly was not a hunter.

Michael watched the capital spending and costs carefully. He spent money when necessary, but didn't throw it around. He never let people take advantage of us. In other words, he was much better at handling money than I was. In the beginning, he asked to see our budget. I told him we had never had one, because to make one for a company like ours was difficult. We bought a new machine only when we got more sustaining business. We improved our facilities when we found it more efficient to do so. I thought we should have a budget when we got bigger, and he agreed.

Sunzi wrote: "The country of which the general is able and the king does not restrain him will win."

During his first year with us, Michael purchased a new mold. He obtained several quotations and decided to order from a shop that had a fairly good reputation and offered a good price. The mold was supposed to be a precision mold. This mold shop was not quite good enough to do such precision work, but I didn't interfere. I figured I was supposed to give him a free hand for ordinary operations like purchasing a mold. If I suggested that another top shop make the mold and we had no problem, he would never realize the pitfall of making a second-grade mold for a precision job. So I let him do his thing.

Unfortunately, we did, eventually, have trouble with that mold.

"We'll never buy molds from this mold shop again," Michael said. In fact, he has been buying high-priced molds whenever feasible ever since.

Confucius said: "If you want to do a good job, you must first sharpen your tools."

To run an efficient operation, we needed all our molds to be in good shape at all times. People sometimes used an imperfect mold for production, when the demand was urgent, but then, the products would not be perfect and the running cycle wouldn't reach capacity. That meant make less profit and maybe even losing money.

Molds are to our business as children are to a family. Never try to save money in educating children, and never try to save money in maintaining molds.

We found that many of our molds needed repair, and Michael brought up the situation with me. Repairing molds in-house was the economical route, but if our tool room tried to fix them all, we would lose production time. I expressed my opinion that all molds should be repaired as soon as possible and kept ready for production at all times. Michael agreed with me and sent many molds to outside mold shops to be repaired.

Nearly a year later, when Michael, Bernie, and I reviewed our annual financial report, the accountant asked, "Why did the mold repair cost shoot up so high last year?"

Michael pointed a finger at me, grinned, and said, "That's John's fault."

We both laughed.

"Right," I said, "but look at the earnings last year."

Of course, we could not attribute the entire increase in revenues to the mold repairs, but I'm certain they were a contributing factor. A well-maintained mold results in a faster cycle and fewer defective products.

The mold repair matter reminded me of a story. Once there was a farmer busy sawing logs. A young student passing by noticed that the sawer was cutting the log very slowly. He said to the farmer, "Sir, you are sawing very slowly. Your saw must need sharpening."

The farmer stood straight up, looked at the young man, pointed at a large pile of logs, and said, "Young man, you see all these logs I have to cut up? How can I have time to sharpen my saw?"

Our president brought us good luck. A couple of years after he joined us, the Kentucky plant gave up in-plant molding and returned to us like a runaway husband returned to his faithful wife. In the three years IBM had tried in-house molding, they had found their attempts to be less economical than buying molded components from outside sources.

The main reason the Kentucky plant gave up in-plant molding was because they had too much trouble producing complicated parts. Their people had only three years of experience, and most outside molders had lived on molding all their lives. When IBM quit molding, they had to dispose of their molding machines. Our president bought two of them at a very good price.

A minor incident occurred that is worth mentioning. One day during a discussion about a new product design, Michael showed me a print made by our engineer. I casually remarked upon the simplification of the company name design on the letterhead logo printed in the title block of the print.

Michael was surprised.

"I noticed it long ago," I said. "I thought you must have seen it and thought it was all right. That's why I never mentioned it."

"Thank you," he said earnestly. "But honestly, I just didn't notice. We'll change it."

This little incident somehow demonstrated to him my sincere intention to give him a free hand in managing the company. Actually, I felt the letter part of the letterhead logo was as important as the picture logo itself. I noticed Michael truly appreciated my consideration and respect for his opinion, and the incident enhanced our trust, friendship, and loyalty to each other.

When Michael finished his first two years with us, I offered to raise his extra earnings bonus from the original contracted two percent to five percent of earnings before taxes. This bonus incentive became a real factor in his earnings and a serious motivation for his performance.

With our president firmly in control, we were in a position to advance or to hold.

Chinese proverb: "To advance, we can afford to take the offense. To hold, we can safely take the defense."

I thought the time had come for us to be aggressive, to take on big jobs requiring large capital investments and to make a vigorous commitment to developing new products.

During a casual conversation with our president, I said, "You know, I have been trying to develop new products all my life. Although I have had some patented proprietary products on the market, we never had anything extraordinary to change the mix of our revenue."

Michael listened, and I continued. "In order for us to grow, I think we have to focus on developing new products."

He thought a moment. "Yes, but that is very difficult."

"As I know only too well," I said. "But that's the only way for us to grow on our own, so we won't have to listen to unreasonable demands from our custom molding customers."

"How true!" he remarked.

After a couple of months, when we were again on the subject of new products, I said to him, "We don't have people who can invent. We have to buy inventions from outside."

He smiled. "I've already contacted an inventors group in New Jersey. I'll visit them next time I go to the East Coast."

I thought that was a very creative move, and, in a few months, we bought two patents, one on a pharmaceutical package, the other a child-resistant closure. Michael negotiated an excellent agreement with the inventors group: We paid a reasonable sum up front and agreed to pay a certain fee every month until we either went into production or dropped the project. If we got to market and made a profit, we would pay the inventors group a small percentage of the revenue.

All child-resistant closures have to pass the protocol, a sample test done with four-year-olds. If they cannot open the closure, the closure is approved. At the same time, the closure must be easy for seniors to operate.

We started working on a pharmaceutical child-resistant package. We made many changes and added important patentable features, while continuing to pay the agreed-upon fees to the inventors. By doing so we reinforced the trust between us. In the future, when they developed new inventions, they would be likely to show us first.

A few months later, during another conversation with Michael about new products, I mentioned the importance of acquisition.

"Maybe we should look seriously into the possibility of acquiring a small plastics company with proprietary products or just buy a product line," I said. "Of course, we will continue to work closely with the inventors group."

Michael answered right away. "I have thought of that already. I'll make some contacts."

Within weeks he found an interesting situation. A good-sized plastics company was for sale, having gone bankrupt trying to develop and market a new product.

"You see how difficult and risky it is to develop new products," I said. "But we have to move forward. Running a company is like paddling a boat upstream. If we cannot push it forward, it will fall backwards by itself."

"I believe that," he said.

Michael Illenberger is the kind of man who gets things done. When he joined us in 1990, we had about thirty molding machines and around one hundred fifty employees working in three continuous shifts. By 1998, he had installed larger and faster machines. In the meantime, through automation, he'd reduced our total personnel to fewer than one hundred forty.

The two latest, most modern machines could produce sixteen plastic tubs in about six seconds, which were inspected, counted, and packed by one operator. I find it interesting to note that these two machines cost about one million dollars. I had started my business on only the fifty-three thousand dollars I collected, plus a thirty thousand dollar loan, and later one investor withdrew three thousand dollars.

We didn't buy the bankrupt company, but we kept our eyes open for inventions as well as acquisitions. I had great faith that, sooner or later, we would have new products going into the market, either from our own creation, from purchasing outside inventions, or from acquisition.

15

New Products

"Spreading on earth is yellow gold, just waiting for a hard-working man."

—Chinese proverb

Although both Michael Illenberger and I firmly believed in the importance of new products, they are not easily created by just anyone at any time. I had worked long and hard to find and develop new products. As I thought back over the years, I recalled that in the 1960s, when I was employed by the research and development group of the can company, I had worked on plastic fittings for tin cans and plastic packaging. At that time, I, privately, hoped to invent something beyond the plastic packaging field for myself, so I might get rich quickly. But like the Chinese proverb says, "Diverting from a trade is like being separated by a mountain." I could not think of anything that might be useful and marketable in any area outside packaging.

After supper, I often sat in front of a small drafting table and thought, but practically nothing of value came to mind. I decided I was not sufficiently acquainted with the market or the preferences of consumers.

After I had my own business for a number of years, I tried to come up with new ideas for plastic products, but the daily problems of the business cluttered my thoughts.

Sunzi wrote: "A wise man considers advantages and disadvantages."

Following his advice, I analyzed the advantages and disadvantages of developing new products. My conclusion was to make survival my first priority and the development of new products secondary.

While running my own business, I also had the opportunity to encourage people to see the disadvantages of inventing.

One day, an older man came to my office and asked me to develop and manufacture an invention of his. This man, obviously a retired blue-collar worker, was casually dressed, had gray-streaked hair, and did not impress me as the intellectual type.

"Thank you for coming in and talking to us," I said to him. "What kind of invention is it?"

"A toy," he answered.

"Are you retired?" I asked.

"Oh, yes."

"What business were you in?"

He said he'd been a foreman with a manufacturing company.

"Do you have a patent on your invention?" I asked.

He said no.

Then, I told him, "Sir, I am a straightforward man, so please don't feel hurt, if I tell you something you won't like to hear. I suggest that you not show your invention to anyone, including me, because you have no patent protection. I do not want to see it until you have protected it."

"But I was sent here by a friend who said I can trust you," he replied.

"I have to protect myself by not seeing it," I answered. "I also want to say that developing an invention is a very expensive process. I suggest you not use your retirement savings for this venture. A new product, particularly a commercial product, is a risky thing. Unless it is extraordinarily good, toy companies won't want to buy from an outside person. You are not a toy expert. You may not know what the public wants at the present time."

He looked startled.

"Think twice before you spend a dollar," I continued. "I do not want to take your money."

He was very disappointed and disheartened. I found it a truly sad situation, but I am glad I told him not to play with his hard-earned savings. He would thank me, if he took my advice.

A couple of years later, another man came to see me about his invention of a hardware item. He seemed to know something about inventions, and had already made mockups and shown them to people. He wore casual clothes and looked healthy. His gray hair implied that he was also a retiree who wanted to get rich, but I couldn't judge his financial situation.

"How do you plan to sell your product?" I asked.

"I think I'll try to sell it to discount houses," he answered readily. "How much would it cost to make a mold to produce small quantities of samples?"

"I do not know about the hardware industry," I said frankly. "But I do know that from concept to commercialization of a new product is a long way and very costly. Maybe you are lucky and have a good thing, but I don't want you spending much money on my work for you. It's too risky. If you insist on trying, you'll have to see some other molder."

He looked surprised.

"You are using your retirement savings, are you?" I asked.

He did not like what I asked, so he said, "You don't like my invention?"

"I cannot judge it. I don't know that business," I answered. "But I do know it is very risky to play with your retirement money."

When he walked out of my office, his good mood did not seem affected by my lack of enthusiasm.

Another time, a middle-aged man came to see me. He had found Magenta in the yellow pages, where we mentioned that we develop new products. He had a job, but had come up with an idea for a household device. He asked me how he should go about bringing it to market.

"You have to develop a device based on your idea," I explained to him. "Only the mechanical features of the device can be patented. So don't tell people about your idea before the features are protected by patent."

He listened, and I continued. "The next thing is to develop your device first. You may tell the idea to me and let me develop your product, if I sign a confidentiality agreement to protect you. But then, the patented features most likely would become my property and not yours. So I'd rather not hear your idea."

This man did look disappointed, when he walked out of my office. But under such conditions, I really did not know how I could help, other than to offer the benefit of my experience. Most people fall in love with their ideas, and when the emotions override the intellect, the situation can be very costly.

As for Magenta, we were better off not getting involved with these inventors. If we had, we would have to tell them how to protect themselves and how to save money every step of the way. We would waste too much time helping them. Amateurs do not know the market's demands, and their inventions most likely would not succeed or make them the fortune they hoped.

By the middle of the 1970s, our business had become better established, and again I turned my attention to the advantages of developing new products. The first person I contacted was a friend of mine who was experienced with health-care laboratory operations. Susan had been a nurse, and later, had supervised hospital laboratories. She had brought me many problems with regard to laboratory apparatus.

Some problems could be easily solved and the apparatuses readily improved, but the improvements were not patentable. If we had already been in the business of manufacturing or selling those apparatuses, we could improve them and increase the sales, but we were not. The best way for us to take advantage of such opportunities would be to buy the company that sold the inferior products. We were not large enough to consider that.

Nevertheless, we began to think about new products seriously. I started to think about closures. Selling tamper-proof closures was less risky than child-resistant closures. When a company manufactures and sells child-resistant closures, it is vulnerable to lawsuits. If anyone gets hurt, child or adult, it is everybody's fault except the one who is hurt, although that is usually the person who did something wrong. The court often makes the manufacturer, the dealer, and the retailer pay dearly.

We concentrated on tamper-proof and tamper-evident closures, and eventually, came up with a tamper-proof liquid pouring spout for metal cans. In the late 1970s, many liquid products were packed in cans, but by the time we were ready for market a few years later, many companies had changed their containers from cans to plastic bottles. We had been working with a vegetable oil company during the development period, but it, too, changed to plastic bottles and dropped our spout.

Fortunately, the can company where I used to work was trying to sell cans to a liquid seasoning manufacturer. In order to beat the competition, they offered their cans with our spout as a complete package. The customer liked the spout, and thus it became the first product of our own sold to a manufacturer.

I experienced indescribable pride at seeing our own product on grocery store shelves. This was a milestone for us. Unfortunately, the quantity this company required was quite small and didn't add much to our revenue.

My next foray into new-product development was directed at health-care products. Generally, manufacturers and marketers liked these products, because if the product cures illness, people are willing to pay dearly for it, and that means a good profit. Another attractive feature is that health-care products are usually used once and then thrown away. This means the usage is large, and the manu-facturer sells more.

I was eager to develop a health-care product when a man walked into my office and demonstrated his intravenous clamp. He claimed his clamp, when put on the intravenous tube, could accurately control the quantity of the dispensed liquid. I was sold then and there.

I negotiated the contract for his patent right. Because of my eagerness, I paid too much money every month to keep the patent right and the development work going, which ensured that he could not take his invention elsewhere.

In the process of perfecting the clamp, we made change after change, sample after sample. We were so close to its being perfect, yet so far away. The situation reminded me of a poker game: Should I give up and stop paying, or should I draw another card?

We had tried more times than I could remember, but we just could not make a perfect clamp. Finally, we realized the clamp would never work well, because the plastic tube on which the clamp is affixed is not perfect in diameter and thickness.

I felt very bad about losing so much money, in addition to so much time. People should never be too anxious for anything.

Chinese proverb: "A large, long range undertaking cannot be done in one day."

What should we do? I wondered. Think!

Many technology companies have think tanks, where employees can brain-storm with a group of creative thinkers. The author of an inspirational book often mentioned sitting in his chair, just thinking. The in-house magazine of a large corporation was called *Think*. Thinking is important. Responsible people should spend more of their working hours thinking instead of mindlessly doing.

One day, I sat in my chair thinking. Suddenly, I picked up the phone and called a friend of mine who owned a reputable plastic designing firm. "You do a lot development work for many companies," I told him. "Is there any new prod-uct with which we can get involved? I mean, is there any invention we can buy or work on?"

"Not at the moment," Gordy answered. "Most of our development jobs are for large corporations." "But," he continued, "I know of an inventor who has a lot of contacts. Why don't you talk to him?"

I invited Gordy's acquaintance to lunch, so we could have time to talk. He didn't have any new inventions, but he invited me to attend a plant tissue culture convention in Philadelphia.

"This is a very new industry," he said, "and it'll need laboratory apparatus for sure."

He explained that plant tissue culture is the process by which a plant is multiplied by using plant tissues, such as roots, instead of seeds. This preserves special features of a plant species and is done by culturing the tissues in a clean laboratory environment.

I was interested and accepted his invitation.

At the convention we met many scientists and PhDs. The inventor introduced me to Dr. Robert Hartman, the director of the Research and Development department of a nursery west of Chicago. I told Dr. Hartman that I wished to develop apparatus for his industry, but knew nothing about plant tissue culture.

"You're welcome to visit my laboratory," he said. "We can talk about what the industry needs."

The next week, I was standing in Dr. Hartman's nursery outside Chicago, listening to him patiently explain each operation in sequence.

"Above everything," he said, "the industry needs a vessel to hold plants without contamination."

After a few weeks and several visits to his laboratory, we came up with a design for a vessel that held promise.

Six months later, we produced a molded model. We showed the vessel model to several laboratories, including Dr. Hartman's. The model turned out not to be suitable at all. It was oversized, expensive, and most importantly, did not seal tightly enough to prevent contamination.

Some of the scientists from the other laboratories reacted with sarcasm, calling it Dr. Hartman's Box, a case of professional jealousy, because they had not gotten a chance to try their hand at developing a vessel. To conceal my own inadequacies as a designer, I told no one, including Dr. Hartman, how much money I had wasted on this box. They would have thought me foolish, if they had known.

I realized I could never develop a usable vessel unless I learned the ins and outs of plant tissue culture operations. I planned to attend the next convention.

Dr. Hartman introduced me to a good number of culture laboratory managers and university professors. They were polite to me, as I was with a culture expert they respected. But when I was alone, some genuinely wished to be friends and others kept their noses in the air. They knew I did not belong to their prestigious profession and was only a product peddler, as they saw it. Of course, I just ignored them.

One time, a sharp-looking lady laboratory manager caught Dr. Hartman and me in front of a meeting hall. Standing about ten feet away, she nodded to us with a playful smile and said in a fairly loud voice, "Do you really intend to sell your box? What do you call it, the Dr. Hartman's box?"

We both smiled back at her, shrugged, and said nothing.

That summer, I made plans to visit as many culture laboratories as possible. Dr. Hartman had moved to Florida and started his own lab, so first I asked him to show me the Florida laboratories. He drove me to all the laboratories in south Florida and introduced me to their owners and managers. After the tour, I had a pretty good idea how a well-run laboratory should be operated. Then he gave me a list of laboratories and university professors in California.

A few weeks later, I took off for California. I visited over twenty laboratories and talked to two professors. Some laboratories were very backward, using milk bottles covered with aluminum foil tied up with rubber bands. One lady manager insisted her lab was doing fine and did not need any efficient apparatus, even though they had many contaminated bottles on the shelves.

After seeing such a variety of laboratory operations, I formulated a pretty good idea of what kind of a vessel we should make. When I returned to my office, I started to design a new one. With the help of Dr. Hartman, we developed one within a few months.

We first tried the vessel in his laboratory. He found it quite satisfactory. Of course, it was not perfect by any means. The cost would have been prohibitive, if we had made a totally contamination-free vessel. We sent samples to other modern laboratories for them to try. The vessel worked well, and we have been selling it ever since. Many went overseas. Now people call the vessel by our company name instead of Dr. Hartman's.

Unfortunately, the plant tissue culture industry did not grow as much as everyone expected. Since much hand labor was involved in the culture operations, the cost to produce young plants ran too high for ordinary crops such as vegetables. Therefore, the culture laboratories mostly produced flowers and ferns. Demand for flowers and ferns were limited, so the industry stalled.

Originally, I'd planned to develop a more sophisticated new generation vessel, but for years the industry had not grown much, and consequently, we dropped the plan. However, we added trays and caps for tubes and jars, and we have been the major supplier of modern plastic apparatus to the plant tissue culture laboratories.

One time, at a convention in Orlando, I invited a group of laboratory managers to dinner. Some indicated I should do that, because I made a lot of money from their laboratories. I was, of course, very gracious, but, at one point, I informed them that the total sales to the laboratories at that time amounted only to about two percent of our total revenue.

During the period around 1980, I went to all the culture conventions to promote our products. At our booth, we ran an educational tape continuously for visitors to watch and showed samples of our products. All in all, I enjoyed it. In various cities in the U.S. we had impressive exhibits, and I made many friends.

At the Tokyo convention, I noticed a different atmosphere. The Japanese respected scholars, professors, and PhDs, just like the Chinese. They did not pay much attention to exhibitors who, they believed, were merely salespeople.

The hotel gave me a room in a small building adjacent to the main hotel. At my insistence, the manager moved me to the main hotel where the exhibits were held. I hired two college girls to help me watch the booth. They loved the job, because they had the opportunity to practice their English conversation.

Near the end of the convention, I was so exhausted that I caught the flu. The manager brought medicine to my room.

My experience at the World Orchid Show of the 1980s in South Africa was a sad one. Although orchid growers from all over the world exhibited beautiful orchids of many varieties, I made a mistake by sharing a booth with a Florida orchid grower who used our vessels to grow young orchids. When we made the arrangement to share the booth over the phone, he sounded okay. But when the exhibition hall opened for visitors, he took over the booth. He tried hard to sell his orchids in our vessels, but never allowed me a chance to talk to visitors who were interested in our vessels. I did not complain to him, as I saw the situation was hopeless.

He was one of a group of visitors from Florida. These five or six couples were typical uneducated Southern farmers, self-satisfied, proud to be Americans, and proud to be white. I felt uncomfortable sitting with them at dinner, as they only talked among themselves. They did not have other exhibits of orchids, and I wondered if they were actually just tourists.

After the show, I joined a safari tour to the National Park of South Africa, hoping to see some wild animals. I rode in a small van with two couples and two other men. The older couple came from Switzerland. They were polite and respectable, but rarely talked to anybody. One man claimed to be a professor from Denmark. He probably was a professor, as he kept his nose in the air all the time toward everyone except the Swiss couple. The other young man was from Australia. He sat in the front seat with the white South African driver. A young couple from New Zealand sat with me in the rear. They had a farm and were very friendly. We stayed together most of the time, when we stopped for meals and sightseeing.

When we stopped at the hotel the first day of the tour, the young Australian stood next to me as the group exited the van. Just to be sociable I tried to talk to him, but he deliberately turned away and ignored me. After that, of course, I never looked at him throughout the tour.

Years ago, I had heard about Australians discriminating against Orientals, but never thought that could happen in the 1980s. Imagine a Chinese-American going all the way to South Africa to be discriminated against by a young Australian bum. All in all, the South Africa exhibit turned out to be a total disaster. I even missed taking a picture of a rare cheetah with a family of four cubs near the end of the safari.

During the 1980s, plant tissue culture was still a young industry, so many professionals, laboratory owners, and equipment suppliers like us hoped one day it would grow, and that in the process we could make some contributions. For many reasons, however, the industry has not prospered so far. We merely maintain the status quo selling our apparatus. Since the industry remained small, it was not worthwhile for others to seriously develop new products to compete with us.

Sunzi wrote: "Not knowing the disadvantages, one cannot know the advantages."

We have found how very difficult and risky it is to develop new products. By buying the plastic closure business from the can company, we gained many patented proprietary closures. The most successful one we developed ourselves was the award-winning sidepour dispenser for powder products. Unfortunately, the sidepour package was intended for snow-melt, but we have had warm weather for years lately. We devoted much time and resources to the plant tissue vessel, but the industry stalled.

All these examples showed me the disadvantages of developing new products. But I also knew how rewarding it could be, if successful. Therefore, Michael and

I plan to keep our focus on the course we have chosen. Our president has already focused on new products as our company strategy, and he has many irons in the fire. Anything we develop or acquire from now on will be the fruit of his efforts.

Chinese proverb: "A good thing goes through many difficulties."

16

Retirement Planning

"Laughter can make you ten years younger."

—Chinese proverb

Besides working on new products, our president has aggressively secured packaging projects and kept our revenue growing. Therefore, by 1997, I felt comfortable enough to plan to see the progress China had made during the eighteen years since I had last visited.

When Helen, Jordan, and I arrived at the Beijing airport, we found it just like an airport in any other country, except more crowded. On the way to the hotel, we saw tall buildings instead of the once-tree-lined road.

The next morning, we walked along a busy commercial street to a major road. People were walking on the sidewalks, bicycles sped by in the bicycle paths, and automobiles moved one after the other in endless lines. Lining the wide streets we could see billboards displaying all kinds of advertisements, mostly of American global companies or Chinese popular products. People were well dressed in colorful Chinese clothing, no gray and blue figures like eighteen years ago. The spirit was upward and cheerful.

We invited our relatives to a feast in one of several modern five-star hotels, a vast improvement over one hotel I had stayed in eighteen years ago, where I had to go to a community washroom to shower. As my brother and his wife had passed away a few years earlier and left no children, all the relatives were from my sister's family, including her son Bo and his family, and her daughter's son Jian and family.

After the dinner we came back to our hotel, and sat in the courtyard around a small table in two rows, with soft drinks for everybody. We talked about our plan to visit my hometown the next day.

Then I said, "It is a Chinese custom for the older family head to give the younger members red packets as acquaintance gifts, and I have just met many of you for the first time. So I am going to ask Jordan write the checks and Jian's daughter, Yuan, to fill in the names and place the checks in the red packets. Then, I'll distribute them to you."

That turned the whole group quiet, and I noticed the waitress was standing straight, looking at me, very amazed. Everyone was probably wondering how big the checks would be. Since Yuan just had a couple of years of English and spent much time to translate the names into English spelling, the whole task took quite a while. When finally, we finished giving the packets, Yuan fell forward on the table with her face buried in both hands. We all laughed loudly. They thanked me, of course, and the waitress relaxed and offered more cold drinks.

Early the next day, Bo, his son-in-law, and Jian and his wife picked us up at the hotel in a van, and we headed for my hometown on the super highway. It took us only two hours instead of the four or five by train I had spent years ago. We turned east on a country road and got the chance to watch farmers harvesting spring wheat.

On the way, Bo said, "I came here a couple of weeks ago to investigate what you might see on your visit. The circled wall is long gone, and buildings have been torn down to widen the streets, so I could not recognize anything. I found an old man, maybe in his seventies, who remembered the old days. He said they tore down your house completely and built a bank there. Fortunately, the rear wall of the house was connected with the outer wall of the alley."

"What does that mean?" I asked.

He said, "Some broken bricks are still on the alley wall. You can take one home as a memory."

We parked the van across the street, and walked through the alley to the rear. Sure enough, interlocked on the wall of the alley, the broken bricks stood out like uneven teeth. I listened to Bo's suggestion and picked a small part of a brick to carry home to the States.

On the way back, we passed through a village where the villagers had built underground shooting stations connected with underground tunnels. Once, they had ambushed a whole platoon of Japanese soldiers, and the soldiers had died without knowing where the bullets came from.

The guide led us down into the tunnel by a steep ladder, and we walked a long distance before we asked the guide to return, as the tunnel was very short and we had to walk with our body and head bent low. We then realized what tremendous hardship the villagers had undergone, and how brave our countrymen had been.

Going back, everyone was tired and silent, but I was busy remembering the town, the streets, the stores, our house, and my parents standing on the steps watching me disappear on the day I left home.

A week later, we invited all my classmates I could remember to a dinner party, and after the dinner, I gave every one a luxurious roller pen with a calculator I had brought with me from the States. Then again, I asked them to take care of themselves and to take walks every day to keep healthy, as I noticed some of them were showing signs of aging.

The next day, we visited my university and were taken on the tour that inspired me to endow the MBA scholarship I described in the opening of this book.

I was invited back to the university for their anniversary celebration in 1998 to participate in the formal establishment of the scholarship in my name. During the celebration I was asked to give a short speech. I told the students to exercise to keep healthy, get rich after graduation, and donate money to our school. The audience applauded and laughed many times during my talk. At the end, they presented me with a videotape of the speech, so I could show it to my wife and son, when I returned home.

As I grew older, my attorney told me I should plan for my family's well being. I engaged a reputable family-planning attorney, who drew up trusts and wills for my wife, my son, and me. These legal protections were important matters. When I got older still, people reminded me about retirement planning. What was I going to do with my business? Sell it or keep it, when and how?

The mail often held flyers from business brokers. "Large corporations want to buy your company," they told me, "and now is a good time to sell your business at a good price and enjoy your retirement years."

I knew quite a few entrepreneurs who had sold their business and retired. The owner of the molding shop who repudiated our verbal royalty agreement sold his business to a large molding company for cash. Then, he oversaw his personal investments from a one-room office in downtown Chicago. I was told he wanted to play it safe and invested all his money in bonds. Over two or three years, the bond market plummeted, he lost a great deal, and not long after, passed away. His plan of selling his business and retiring might have been all right, had he invested wisely and safely.

My business had slowly expanded year after year. Magenta had enjoyed growth in revenue, in its fine reputation, and in the size of the facility. How could I be sure the next owner would want to keep the business going and not let it run down? I certainly would hate to see someone ruin the company or its reputation, or even make its name or signature color disappear. When a large corporation bought out a small company, they usually merged the operations into their various groups until the small company disappeared.

Also, my business was a safe haven for my family. My wife would always have a reliable income, and my son would be free to venture into whatever direction he chose. If he succeeded, all the better, but if not, he could count on Magenta as a secure shelter for future generations. This financial safety net was already in place. What degree of effort would I need to expend to build a new one? A family shelter is not easy to build and should not be torn down lightly.

I had another concern: If I sold my business and collected a large sum for it, what would I do with the money? This situation confronted a friend of mine who owned a nice restaurant. Someone walked in and offered him a very good price to buy it. He requested my advice.

"What are you going to do with the money besides paying taxes?" I asked him.

"I probably will open another restaurant," he answered without hesitation.

"How much money would you need to open a restaurant like this one?" I inquired.

He thought a moment. "About the same amount of money I would get for this one." A big smile spread across his face. "Oh, I see what you mean." He did not sell his restaurant.

Other investments normally would include stocks and real estate, but I could never be a landlord. Learning about real estate would be like starting a new business, and that is not for retirement.

As for bonds, I never knew much about them, but did realize that investing in stock is riskier than most people believe. In short, with a large sum of cash I would have to work on investments. To work on making money is not what retirement means.

Finally, what would happen to my employees, if I sold my business? In the best scenario, the new management would run the company without making any changes. But some of my workers might not like the new owner or vice versa. How could I put them into such a position after they had worked for me for so many years? What if they lost their profit-sharing fund, after working for me for so many years?

After nearly thirty years of hard work and dedication to build a secure future for my family and my employees, how could I think of giving away my baby to somebody else?

I thought the safest thing to invest in was my own business, as that was what I knew best. That would mean someone would have to manage it after I retired.

Fortunately, I was lucky enough to have an excellent president already in control of my company. This is truly a blessing for me, my family, my employees, and for Michael Illenberger himself. He feels secure, as he knows the business will not be sold. Since he has done a beautiful job, I offered him a deferred compensation plan, so that when he retires at the age of seventy, he will be a millionaire, even if our company does not grow anymore. In the meantime, I suggested that he start looking for someone, such as a chief engineer or a vice president, who can be developed to become his successor.

As for me, my daily life was never an issue with regard to retirement. I can always find interesting projects to keep myself busy or do things I enjoy. One major concern that did come to my mind was, who would be my friends after I left the business arena?

Chinese proverb: "The bitterest thing for people is to be lonely when old."

Confucius said: "Having a friend coming from afar, how happy I am!"

When people get older, most of their friends are scattered all over, and some might have passed away. Three of my personal friends had been business friends years ago, but two had passed away, and the other moved out of state. Getting together with him is difficult.

The most disheartening thing is that most business friends do not evolve into personal friends after retirement. In fact, many business friends abandoned me as soon as I transferred the daily operational responsibilities to our new president.

One of my banker friends got along well with me for many years, but stopped having lunch with me, when Mr. Illenberger took charge. Shortly thereafter, this banker bought a condo and hosted a housewarming party. "Why did he invite our president and his wife but leave me out?" I wondered. I really had believed we were pretty good friends.

Similarly, an attorney, who had worked for Magenta for many years, had become my friend, as had our families. One time, we invited them for dinner, and at the evening's end, he said, "John, we want to invite you and your family to your favorite restaurant near our office. I'll call you."

Months later, after the attorney learned that Mr. Illenberger was running the whole show, he came to our office to get acquainted. The three of us sat at a square table during lunch. Michael took a chair to his right and I to his left. During the whole lunch the attorney faced right and talked to Michael continuously. Only when I asked questions, did he face me a couple of times.

Near the end of the meeting, he invited Michael and his wife, together with my wife and me, to dinner, then turned toward me again, and said, "At your favorite restaurant." We both turned him down, and I did it for good. All those years, I had misjudged him as a personal friend.

Dinner invitations alone cannot prove friendship, but the attitude and intention do. These events made me wonder if I had not been sincere or if business friends were supposed to be only for business.

Stung from these experiences, I could not help but wonder who I would spend time with when I retired. I'm lucky that both my wife and son are quite a bit younger than I, and I'll have them as friends when I grow old. But how about them? I often remind them to cultivate true friendships among relatives, schoolmates, and coworkers, so they will be surrounded by loving friends, when they get old, not like the business friends I have made during the years.

I am often asked, "Are you saving Magenta for your son to run one day?" The answer is no. After he graduates from college, I do not want Jordan to work at my company to learn about the business world. How could anyone work and learn at a place where everyone knows he is the boss's son? Nobody would give him a hard time. A person learns better, if he gets into trouble occasionally.

Magenta is not large. If Jordan shows a flair for business, I wouldn't want him to be limited by the size of my company. I prefer to let him make his own future and do whatever he likes, with my help if needed. I would like to see him working for some other well-managed company for a few years after he finishes college. If he has good ideas and the desire to try his hand, I'll give him capital to start his own enterprise. People learn the most, when they run their own company.

I never worried about money. If Jordan lost money in a venture, I would give him the capital to try again. After all, I failed in my first try.

Chinese proverb: "To leave the son a thousand pieces of gold is not as good as teaching him a profession."

I don't believe that children must start from the bottom to learn about life. People can learn about life at any level. Why not let Jordan take advantage of having a successful father? I could have built a much larger company than our current one, if I'd had more capital to start with. I wouldn't have spent ten years struggling for survival. I will help my son in whatever way I can before and after my retirement. Of course, he should be honest and do things that are beneficial to society.

My investors have also benefited from my hard work and their decision to have faith in me. Nearly twenty years after I started Magenta, my schoolmate-stockholder, Joe Wang, requested that I buy back his shares. His elder son required a kidney operation, and they needed extra money. The company paid him the right amount for his shares based on a generous calculation by my accountant.

Naturally, he and his family were happy about the returns, but I wished he could have held onto those shares a few years longer. Our company would be worth more, and a much larger amount would have been paid to his family.

Not long after that transaction, my coworker-stockholder retired and wanted money for his shares. He was so happy with the return on his investment that, according to a mutual friend, he went out and bought a brand new Cadillac on the spot.

These stock buy-backs were good for the company, also. My schoolmate had three sons, none of whom I knew well. What was I going to do with these new investors, if they inherited our company stock?

The two stock buy-backs reminded me of the shares held by Mr. Fu, my friend in New York. He had no family, and I presumed he would donate his assets to charity and possibly, our company stock to his church. What was I going to do with a church stockholder?

With everyone getting older, I telephoned Mr. Fu and asked what he planned to do with his stock. He said he hadn't thought about it. I told him the other investors had sold their shares to the company.

"This reminded me of your shares," I said. "I thought you might donate them to your church. I think it's much simpler for you to leave money with your church than the stock of a privately held small company."

He agreed. We paid him according to our formula, which was more generous than the practice on Wall Street. Soon, I received a letter from him that read in part: "I am deeply moved by your fairness and kindness to me that I will never forget."

In the beginning, this man had refused to invest money in my venture until I telephoned him four times, and later he turned down my request for more help. Since we had been friends for over twenty years at that time, my feelings were so deeply hurt that I promised myself I would definitely make money for him. And so I did. So far as my stockholders are concerned, I have a clear conscience.

In the late years of my life, I would prefer to give money to relatives or friends while I am still alive. I do not wish to have relatives waiting for an inheritance after my death. So far, I have given different amounts to more than twenty close schoolmates and relatives under various circumstances.

After Joe Wang had heart surgery, I sent him a check and asked him to buy old hens to make a heavy chicken broth for recovery. Later Mrs. Wang told me that Joe had framed the check in a small picture frame and hung it in the bedroom for private memory.

I also like to make donations to institutions, preferably schools or universities.

Confucius said: "A gentleman despises not leaving behind a name when he is gone."

Personally, I don't care about the name; after I'm gone, I won't know one way or another, but I hope my examples of philanthropy will inspire future generations.

Once, I donated money to a zoo to build a new section of a building. They put my name, along with other donors, on the wall. One summer day, I went to the zoo with my son and showed him my name. We both felt pretty proud of it. I hope that memory will inspire him to give generously in the future.

A donation I made to a Chicago museum came about indirectly, because I was angry with one of my foremen. Whitie frequently failed to follow the mold trial procedure. One time, his failure wasted two days' production time. I called him to my office and said, "Whitie, you make me sick! I'm not going to say anything anymore."

Then, I put on my jacket and told Geri, "I'm going to the museum to get rid of my anger. I'll be back in a couple of hours."

After an hour of wandering around the exhibits, I decided to return to my office, but I couldn't find my car in the parking lot. It had been stolen.

The next day, I called the museum administration and suggested they install a guard booth at the parking lot entrance. A couple of weeks later, I received a phone call from a Mr. Chelf, the museum's head of development, inviting me for tour of the background activities of the museum and lunch. I accepted the invitation, because from the beginning, I intended to help with the guard booth project.

During the lunch, I offered to donate half the cost of installing a suitable guard booth at the entrance of the parking lot in front of the beautiful museum building. Mr. Chelf thought it was a good idea.

Two months later, however, I received a letter from Mr. Chelf saying that the museum management had decided to buy a movable booth from a catalog, at half the estimated cost of constructing a stationary booth. He asked me to pay the entire cost of the small booth.

This was not what I had in mind, and I told him the museum should have a prestigious guard booth to suit the gigantic, classical entrance of the magnificent building. When Mr. Chelf replied he could not reverse the management's decision, I sent him a check for the booth.

The next time, I visited the museum I saw the tiny booth on wheels, and I just laughed. How could they have placed such a cheap-looking booth in front of such a grand museum?

Although I felt disappointed by the museum's management, I still prefer to put money directly in the hands of the people who need it, particularly for education. I don't feel comfortable donating to organizations that distribute the money for me, although I do understand that some of those organizations have done great work to help people all over the world.

Conclusion

"One who has will, will succeed."

—Chinese proverb

When the Japanese took Taiwan from China nearly a hundred years ago, they encouraged the smart Chinese students to become medical doctors by setting the payment standard much higher than for other professionals. Doctors are not likely to lead a revolt.

After Taiwan returned to Chinese rule, families there still preferred their daughters to marry doctors. If the parents thought such a match would provide financial abundance, they were mistaken. Doctors' incomes were fixed amounts, no matter what service they might provide. For example, an operation might cost thousands of dollars, but the surgeon would be paid by each operation.

A surgeon could increase his income only by performing more operations. The way the system worked, a successful restaurateur's income could be greater than a surgeon's. The physician, however, enjoyed job security and did not have to be enterprising or take financial risks.

Chinese proverb: "An able man doesn't make a fixed-amount income."

Therefore, I often encourage young men to be entrepreneurs. If they fail, they can always try again. If they succeed, their earning potential is unlimited. The machines they own can be making money for them, while they look for more customers.

To help young people advance in their career, I share the stories of my own experience as written in my book, as reference and inspiration.

What qualities do you need to be successful? I have been told that most entrepreneurs have inherited their business aptitude, but I'm not sure how true that is. My grandfather was a successful entrepreneur, but my father and great-grandfather were not.

In my opinion, a strong basic education is essential. Many businesses do not require an advanced degree or college education, but I believe that without at least a good high school education, an entrepreneur will probably have difficulty managing a large and growing business.

Whatever the level of their diploma, all entrepreneurs must work hard. They also think hard, day and night. In my youth, I lugged away tree stumps, clearing farmland under the roasting Georgia sun. It was a back-breaking job, but hard work does not hurt anybody.

The toughest task for any entrepreneur is perhaps raising enough money to open and sustain a new business. Saving money is very difficult for salaried people; they need their limited income to meet their personal needs. I was an average engineer, and naturally, my friends and relatives had modest incomes also. I collected only $53,000 to start my business, and $3,000 was withdrawn by one investor. Nevertheless, entrepreneurs should do their best to borrow as much money as possible and move forward with the venture with whatever they have; otherwise, the venture will never get started.

Unless you have some special innovation or market niche, venture-capital people probably will not be interested in your endeavor, so borrowing is the only choice. Through perseverance I was awarded a $30,000 government-guaranteed bank loan.

Convincing friends to invest in you requires that you establish your trustworthiness, a quality that is the essence of Confucius's teachings. How we interact begins to define itself during childhood. We establish our trustworthiness with our little friends on the playground, and later with our schoolmates, and then our coworkers. When people around us know our word of honor is as bankable as gold, then, we can ask them to take a chance on us with their money.

What business to choose depends on the entrepreneur. Every person and situation is unique, and we have to pick our own specialty. A field with large potential has obvious advantages over one that cannot grow big. Whether a business is large or small, the owner must work long hours, think all the time, and worry about everything. So why not choose something that eventually offers greater rewards?

Once business is started, the entrepreneur should, setting himself as an example, begin to build the company culture, emphasizing modern management methods and adopting Eastern wisdom to set up a right course for progress and growth.

Confucius said: "Gentleman should not seek petty gains."

I firmly believe that to run a business operation, you should concentrate on making the enterprise a success and not worry about counting your pennies. Don't waste your time and energy trying to find the best deal or the cheapest price. The value gained won't be worth it. Instead, you should spend the time and energy on getting new customers or improving operational efficiency. Your rewards will be greater in the end.

Attract desirable customers through communication and understanding, excellent service, and fair price. A good salesperson always knocks on doors, talks to customers face-to-face, and uses the telephone only for making arrangements. Nobody wants to buy anything except basic commodities from a stranger.

Chinese proverb: "hearing about hundred times is not as good as seeing once."

Keep customers happy by delivering quality products on time at competitive prices and maintaining truthful communications. At Magenta, if I could not deliver good products on time due to faulty tools, I kept my customer informed. Never hide the truth; customers do not like to be surprised. Customers are human, too, and they will cooperate if they believe you have done all you could and have told the truth.

I like to emphasize that loyalty still works. Both Confucius and Mencius advised people to be benevolent. Suppliers will give you reliable service if they know you are loyal to them. Engineers, consultants, accountants, attorneys, all will render honest services, if you demonstrate loyalty. They consistently act in your best interest, if they believe their efforts are worthwhile and appreciated.

Similarly, loyal employees are reliable workers. If they know the company is loyal to them, they will be loyal to the company. Everyone has to make a living and looks for betterment in life. If you try your best to help people reach their goals, they will become loyal employees.

Mencius said: "To convince people by virtue, people, delighted in the heart, will be persuaded sincerely."

To make your company a success, you need employees who are intelligent, capable, honest, and loyal. In the beginning, when my company was small, all the people I hired were honest and nice. For years, we built a culture with a family atmosphere. I enjoyed good relations with my employees, except for three or four law-abusing cases.

When Magenta grew larger, some of our management personnel showed limited capabilities, and our president considered the situation urgent. I suggested that he add capable new people to build a powerful new team in a few years, and use our older managers to do less important tasks.

Personnel must be intelligent to learn new things, create new ideas, and keep up with the growth of the company. Always hire the best available; in the long run, the best is the cheapest.

Follow the same principle, for machinery and equipment, also buy the best you can afford. The best equipment will make more money, even though the initial outlay is greater than lesser quality materials. Remember, Confucius advised people to use sharpened tools.

The entrepreneur meets many kinds of people, some more likable than others. In any case, never make an enemy, you never know when you'll meet the person again, at a time, when he can really hurt or help you. Make friends with those you like and keep your distance from those you do not like.

Resolve disputes by discussing, negotiating, and creating options agreeable to both parties. Sit at a square or round table, with both parties next to each other at ninety degrees, not opposing each other. Have pens and paper ready. Write down what each party wants to have, then, quietly think of options to satisfy as much as possible the requirements of both parties.

Here's a Western saying: "There are a million ways to skin a cat." Working together, the parties should be able to come up with a solution that makes no one a winner or a loser. In this way both are winners, because they do not have to go to court and pay huge legal fees, and neither has created an enemy. I paid off a blackmailer with a negotiated sum rather than hiring a detective and going to court. I bought our third building, while sitting ninety degrees from the seller at a lunch table. Of course, like Sunzi wrote, you have to know what both you and your opponent really want.

Businesses have their ups and downs, but make sure you don't drift into a crisis, like I did. I should never have allowed IBM to become so crucial to Magenta's stability. When IBM decided to do its own molding, I had to depend upon myself to overcome the crisis. And if a friend had not told me about the closure business of the can company, I would have been set back at least three years. Never let one company control your financial well-being.

Chinese proverb: "Experiencing one event will gain one notch of wisdom."

Some entrepreneurs want to hold on to their authority, recognizing that no one will work for you the way he would work for himself. However, you can transfer authority if you offer great incentives. Chinese proverb supports this truth and I have found it to be correct. The successful entrepreneur should plan early for his or her successor. Many entrepreneurs hate to let go of authority. This is not wise. Sooner or later, we all must let go.

Likewise, pay employees according to their value to you. You don't lose anything if you pay people what you think they are worth.

During the last thousand years, China has lost the spirit of creation and risk-taking in her culture. That is why I advised the MBA scholarship receivers to apply what they learned in school on Western modern management theories. At the same time, they should lead people to adopt Eastern wisdom, while they build their organization's culture.

Almost all I have said pertains to showing people how to build flourishing businesses. To have complete success, to be a successful person, in addition to accomplishment in business, you need health and happiness. I have always referred to the Eastern wisdom sayings quoted throughout this book. They truly can give you new outlook to life, and peace of mind, happiness, and good health.

Chinese proverb: "Missing by a hair, result will differ by thousand miles."

To all my readers, I wish you success in wealth, health, and happiness. Since time is more valuable than money, may I offer one more proverb:

"One inch of time is worth one inch of gold. One inch of gold cannot buy one inch of time."

0-595-30593-8